Cambridge Elements

Elements in Forensic Linguistics
edited by
Tim Grant
Aston University
Tammy Gales
Hofstra University

THE LANGUAGE OF FAKE NEWS

Jack Grieve
University of Birmingham and Alan Turing Institute
Helena Woodfield
University of Birmingham

CAMBRIDGE
UNIVERSITY PRESS

Shaftesbury Road, Cambridge CB2 8EA, United Kingdom

One Liberty Plaza, 20th Floor, New York, NY 10006, USA

477 Williamstown Road, Port Melbourne, VIC 3207, Australia

314–321, 3rd Floor, Plot 3, Splendor Forum, Jasola District Centre,
New Delhi – 110025, India

103 Penang Road, #05–06/07, Visioncrest Commercial, Singapore 238467

Cambridge University Press is part of Cambridge University Press & Assessment,
a department of the University of Cambridge.

We share the University's mission to contribute to society through the pursuit of
education, learning and research at the highest international levels of excellence.

www.cambridge.org
Information on this title: www.cambridge.org/9781009349130

DOI: 10.1017/9781009349161

First published 2023

A catalogue record for this publication is available from the British Library.

ISBN 978-1-009-34913-0 Paperback
ISSN 2634-7334 (online)
ISSN 2634-7326 (print)

The Language of Fake News

Elements in Forensic Linguistics

DOI: 10.1017/9781009349161
First published online: March 2023

Jack Grieve
University of Birmingham and Alan Turing Institute

Helena Woodfield
University of Birmingham

Author for correspondence: Jack Grieve, j.grieve@bham.ac.uk

Abstract: In this Element, the authors introduce and apply a framework for the linguistic analysis of fake news. They define fake news as news that is meant to deceive as opposed to inform and argue that there should be systematic differences between real and fake news that reflect this basic difference in communicative purpose. The authors consider one famous case of fake news involving Jayson Blair of *The New York Times*, which provides them with the opportunity to conduct a controlled study of the effect of deception on the language of a single reporter following this framework. Through a detailed grammatical analysis of a corpus of Blair's real and fake articles, this Element demonstrates that there are clear differences in his writing style, with his real news exhibiting greater information density and conviction than his fake news. This title is also available as Open Access on Cambridge Core.

Keywords: disinformation, discourse analysis, corpus linguistics, forensic linguistics, natural language processing

ISBNs: 9781009349130 (PB), 9781009349161 (OC)
ISSNs: 2634-7334 (online), 2634-7326 (print)

Contents

Series Preface

The *Elements in Forensic Linguistics* series from Cambridge University Press publishes across four main topic areas (1) investigative and forensic text analysis; (2) the study of spoken linguistic practices in legal contexts; (3) the linguistic analysis of written legal texts; (4) explorations of the origins, development and scope of the field in various countries and regions. *The Language of Fake News* by Jack Grieve and Helena Woodfield is situated in the first of these and examines whether there are observable linguistic differences between fake news and genuine news articles.

Jack Grieve is best known for bringing quantitative and corpus methods to a variety of linguistic questions such as dialectology, language change, and authorship analysis methods. His quantitative work always brings linguistic insights and understanding to the fore and here with Helena Woodfield, whose principal area of research is fake news, they together bring this approach to the natural experiment provided by the Jayson Blair episode at *The New York Times.*

Jayson Blair was accused of and admitted falsifying a large number of news stories at *The New York Times,* and a subsequent inquiry by the paper identified the bad, and by implication, the good stories for the relevant period of his employment. For Grieve and Woodfield this creates parallel corpora ripe for exploration. Their principal insight is that as fake news and real news have distinctive communicative functions, respectively to deceive and to inform, the language used to carry these functions will also differ. In this Element they set out to identify and describe those differences. The implication of this approach is that linguistic analysis, independently from fact-checking approaches, can make an important contribution to fake news detection.

This sets up a new research agenda for linguistic fake news detection, which can be further explored, perhaps in future Cambridge Elements.

Tim Grant
Series Editor

1 Introduction

1.1 The Problem of Fake News

There is no simple definition of fake news. The term can be used to refer to any news that is suspected to be inaccurate, biassed, misleading, or fabricated. This includes news originating from across the news media landscape, from anonymous blogs to mainstream newspapers. The term is often used by the public, politicians, and the news media to attack news, journalists, and news outlets deemed to be problematic. It is even common for allegations of fake news made by one outlet to be labelled as fake news by another. During the 2016 American presidential election, Hillary Clinton, the Democrats, and the mainstream press claimed that fake news from social media accounts, right-wing news outlets, and foreign governments was propelling Donald Trump to victory, while Trump, the Republicans, and the right-wing press claimed that Clinton, the Democrats, and the mainstream press were spreading fake news about these and other scandals to undermine Trump's campaign (Allcott & Gentzkow 2017). Fake news became the focus of the news, with news organisations arguing over whose news was faker.

Given this situation, how can the public judge what news is real and what news is fake? We cannot trust the news media to lead public inquiry into its own practices, nor can we trust the government or industry to monitor the news media, as they are most often the subject of the news whose validity is being debated. Academic research on fake news is therefore especially important, but it is also difficult to conduct (Lazer et al. 2018). Researchers must define fake news in a specific and meaningful way and then apply this definition to identify instances of real and fake news for analysis. This is a challenging task. Any piece of news communicates a wide range of information, some of which can be true, some of which can be false, and all of which can be an opinion. Often the only way to verify if news is real or fake is to conduct additional independent investigation into the events being covered. Crucially, even if fake news is defined precisely and in a way that is acceptable to most people, researchers must still label individual pieces of news as fake that a substantial proportion of the public believe are real. The study of fake news therefore quickly becomes politicised, further eroding public confidence, and encouraging researchers to define fake news in such a way that data can be collected easily and uncontroversially, often moving research further away from the central problem of fake news.

To understand the central problem of fake news, it is important to consider the history of fake news. Although most current research focuses on the very recent phenomenon of online fake news, reviewing the history of deception in the news media can help researchers understand what communicative events are considered fake news, how these different forms of fake news are related, and which types of fake news should be of greatest scholarly concern. The history of fake news can also point us to specific cases for further analysis, depoliticising the study of fake news by allowing researchers to focus on news coverage of events that are of less immediate consequence.

The history of fake news is almost as old as the history of news itself. In Europe, the precursor to the modern newspaper were the *avvisi*, handwritten political newsletters from Italy that circulated across the continent during the sixteenth and seventeenth centuries (Infelise 2002). Unlike personal letters, the *avvisi* were intended to report general information and to be widely read. Unsurprisingly, we can find reports almost immediately of authorities questioning the veracity of the information being presented and the motives of their authors, who were generally anonymous. For example, in 1570, Pope Pius V executed one suspected author, Niccolo Franco, for defaming the church. Alternatively, the Italian scholar Girolamo Frachetta considered whether the *avvisi* could be used in wartime to spread false information to the enemy in his 1624 political treatise *A Seminar on the Governance of the State and of War* (Infelise 2002).

Indeed, there are many cases of fake news being used to mislead foreign populations and governments, exactly as Frachetta suggested. Many historical examples come from the Cold War, especially the Soviet use of *dezinformatsiya*, the purposeful spread of false information, which was often spread via the foreign press (Cull et al. 2017). The word *disinformation* only entered the English language in the 1980s due to increased awareness of so-called *active measures*, a wide range of strategies used by the USSR for undermining foreign countries, including fake news. One of the most famous of these initiatives was 'Project Infektion', which involved the Soviets spreading rumours that the United States had engineered AIDS, initiated by a letter published in an obscure Indian newspaper in 1983, titled 'AIDS may invade India: Mystery disease caused by US experiments' (Boghardt 2009).

It is perhaps more common, however, for fake news during wartime to be directed at one's own citizens – to encourage support for war and to manage expectations. For example, during World War I, the Committee on Public Information was established in the United States to influence the media and shape popular opinion, especially as President Woodrow Wilson had campaigned on staying out of the war (Hollihan 1984). Similar strategies were used to promote the Vietnam and Iraq wars. Most notably, we now know that reporting on the presence of weapons of mass destruction in Iraq after 9/11 was fabricated to build support for the war, especially to help Tony Blair justify the United Kingdom joining the coalition (Robinson 2017).

Fake news is not new, but the nature of fake news has shifted in recent years due to the growth of digital communication and social media (Lazer et al. 2018). The Internet has changed the medium over which news is published and accessed by the public. Consequently, people now have access to a much wider range of news sources, which disseminate information continuously throughout the day, often from very specific perspectives, while social media provides a platform for people worldwide to share and discuss the news. One important effect of this new approach to the production and consumption of news is that people can focus exclusively on the information they want to hear, leading to what has become known as the *echo chamber* (Del Vicario et al. 2016). The rise of blogging and social media has also given the opportunity to people from outside the mainstream news media to spread their own message, including potentially fake news.

This type of online fake news has been the focus of much concern in recent years, including in the lead up to the 2016 US Election. Perhaps the most notorious example was the 'Pizzagate' conspiracy theory, which went viral in 2016, after Wikileaks published the personal emails of John Podesta, Clinton's campaign manager (Kang 2016). Extremist websites and social media accounts reported that the emails contained coded messages related to a satanic paedophile ring involving high-ranking officials, which allegedly met at various locations, including the Comet Ping Pong pizzeria in Washington. Provoked by these reports, a man travelled to the nation's capital from North Carolina, shooting at the pizzeria with a semi-automatic rifle. The Covid pandemic also offers numerous examples of this type of online fake news (see van Der Linden et al. 2020). For example, social media has been used to spread fake news about alternative treatments for Covid that are potentially deadly, including ingesting bleach (World Health Organization 2020).

Although it seems reasonable to assume that the amount of fake news has increased in recent years, we should not assume that the effect of fake news has become worse. Most notably, reporting from the mainstream news media leading up to the second Iraq War, which predates the rise of social media, was arguably far more damaging than anything that has happened since. In some ways, social media has even made it more difficult for certain types of fake news to spread by increasing public scrutiny of the news media and by amplifying alternative perspectives. An important example is coverage of the murder of George Floyd in May 2020. This event was filmed by a teenager named Darnella Frazier, who was walking to the store for groceries. She posted the video on social media, giving rise to widespread public protest to police brutality towards African Americans – a topic often overlooked by mainstream news media, which can be considered an example of fake news by omission (Wenzel 2019). In recognition of the importance of this act, which was only made possible by the existence of these non-traditional platforms for sharing information, Frazier received a Pulitzer Prize in 2021.

Overall, the problem of fake news is long-standing, pervasive, and potentially of great consequence, even leading to war. The study of fake news is therefore of true societal importance. Fake news is also very diverse, driven by a wide range of specific political, social, economic, and individual factors. In addition, it is clear that fake news, at least in its most troubling instantiations, is not simply characterised by inaccurate reporting: it is intentionally dishonest, designed to deceive as opposed to inform the public.

In this Element, we therefore adopt the view that fake news is most productively analysed as *deceptive news*, in contrast with most academic research on fake news, which focuses on *false news*. In other words, we define fake news based on the intent of the author: as opposed to real news, whose primary goal is to inform readers about new and important information that the journalist believes to be true, the goal of fake news is to deceive the public, to make them believe information that the journalist believes to be false. This approach not only forces us to concentrate on the most problematic forms of fake news, but, as we argue, it provides a more meaningful basis for the analysis of the *language* of fake news, which is the subject of this Element.

1.2 Fake News and Linguistics

Understanding the language of fake news is key to understanding the problem of fake news because most cases of fake news *are* language. Fake news can involve pictures and other media, but usually an instance of fake news consists primarily of a *news text* – an article in a newspaper, a report on the radio, a post on social media, an interview on television. The news text is the basic communicative unit of journalism and consequently the basic unit of analysis in most research on fake news. The main questions we pursue in this Element are therefore how can the language of fake news be analysed in a meaningful way? How can we describe linguistic differences between news texts that are real and news texts that are fake? And how can we understand why this variation exists?

Crucially, however, we should not assume that the language of real and fake news differs systematically. There has been considerable research in natural language processing (Oshikawa et al. 2020) where machine learning models are trained to automatically distinguish between real and fake news based on patterns of language use, often achieving relatively high levels of accuracy. This may seem like evidence of variation between the language of real and fake news, but it is important to consider these results with care, especially as this research prioritises the maximisation of classification accuracy over the explanation of patterns of language use. There are two basic reasons for caution. First, the data upon which these systems are trained and evaluated may not isolate variation between real and fake news, especially given the inherent challenges associated with defining these terms and identifying cases of each. Second, these systems often focus more on variation in language *content* than variation in language *structure*: the identification of *topical* trends that tend to distinguish between real and fake news is different from the identification of *stylistic* variation in the language of real and fake news regardless of topic. In other words, research in natural language processing focuses on the *language* of fake news, but it does not necessarily focus on the *linguistics* of fake news.

Although linguistic perspectives on fake news are limited, fake news is fundamentally a linguistic phenomenon, and its analysis should therefore be grounded in linguistic theory. To address this basic limitation with fake news research, we propose a framework for the linguistic analysis of fake news in this Element. Our framework is based on functional theories of language use, drawing especially on research on register variation (Biber & Conrad 2019), which has repeatedly demonstrated that differences in communicative purpose and context are reflected in linguistic structure. In addition, our framework is based on the distinction between misinformation and disinformation (Rubin 2019), which we believe is crucial for understanding what fake news is and why the language of real and fake news should differ. By bringing together these two perspectives for the first time, we provide a basis for the linguistic analysis of fake news – for collecting real and fake news texts, for comparing their grammatical structure, and for understanding why this structure varies depending on whether their author intends to inform or deceive.

To demonstrate how our framework can be used to better understand the language of fake news, in this Element, we focus on one especially famous episode drawn from the history of the news media. This case involves Jayson Blair, a young reporter at *The New York Times*, who published a series of fabricated news articles in the early 2000s (Hindman 2005). In addition to its notoriety, this case is especially well suited for the linguistic analysis of fake news for three reasons. First, there is a relatively large amount of real and fake news available from one author and from the same time period, which has been validated through an extensive investigation by *The New York Times* (Barry et al. 2003) and acknowledged by Blair himself (Blair 2004). This gives us a controlled context for the study of fake news, where we have substantial amounts of comparable and valid real and fake news data, allowing us to effectively isolate the effects of deception on the language of one journalist. Second, we know much about why Blair wrote fake news, including from his own account and the account of *The New York Times,* giving us a basis for explaining differences in language use that we observe. Third, this case is relatively uncontroversial, as it is old enough that everyone can agree that the articles in question were faked, regardless of their political outlook – an important factor that has often limited the societal impact of fake news research. In addition, the case reminds us that fake news can be found across the news media, including in one of the most respected newspapers in the world.

The analysis of the language of fake news grounded in linguistic theories and methods also opens up the possibility for a wide range of applications. Although our goal is not to develop systems for fake news detection, the most obvious application of our research is to support the language-based identification of fake news. Most notably, this includes considerable current research in natural language processing concerned with developing systems for automatically classifying real and fake news at scale via supervised machine learning (Oshikawa et al. 2020). As noted above, these systems can achieve good results, but they are not designed to explain why the language of real and fake news differs, and they appear to focus more on the content of fake news than its linguistic structure (Castelo et al. 2019). Our framework is not intended to supplant these types of systems, but it can offer an explanation for why they work, or why they might appear to work, which is necessary to justify the real-world application of such tools. Furthermore, the identification of a principled set of linguistic features for the analysis of real and fake news can be used to enhance existing machine learning systems, which tend to be based on relatively superficial feature sets like the use of individual words and word sequences. These types of insights can be especially useful to improve performance on more challenging cases, which also seem likely to be the most important cases of fake news. In addition, our framework can directly inform how fake news corpora should be compiled in a principled manner for the robust training and evaluation of fake news detection systems, which is a major limitation in much current research on fake news (Asr & Taboada 2018).

The framework we propose is also of direct value to the detailed discursive analysis of individual cases of fake news of sufficient importance to warrant close attention. For example, in a legal context, empirical analysis presented as evidence in court is often required to be based on accepted scientific theory (Allen 1993). Until now, however, there has been no clear explanation for why the linguistic structure of real and fake news should be expected to differ systematically. Our framework also potentially provides a basis for extending discourse analytic methods for deception detection more generally in forensic linguistics, which is relevant across a wide range of areas, including for police interviews (Picornell 2013). In addition, our framework can be of value for supporting work in *investigative linguistics*, which is an emerging field of applied linguistics that focuses on the application of methods for the study of language use to make sense of real-world issues currently in the news (Grieve & Woodfield 2020).

More generally, understanding the language of fake news, and how it differs from the language of real news, is important for understanding the language of the news media, and, through this language, the biases and ideologies that underlie any act of journalism. The current fake news crisis reflects a growing and general distrust of the news media that cannot be rectified simply by developing systems for automatically detecting real and fake news with a reasonable degree of accuracy. An article that obliquely expresses the editorial view of a newspaper in a context that appears to be purely informational is not necessarily fake, but it has real societal consequences. Being able to recognise the motivations of journalists and news outlets through the analysis of their language is an important part of reading the news intelligently and holding the news media accountable. Studying the discourse of fake news is therefore part of the greater enterprise of understanding the expression of information, opinion, and prejudice in the news media – understanding how the language of the news media shapes the world around us and our perceptions of it. We therefore hope that our framework will also be valuable for the critical analysis of the news media (van Dijk 1983).

Finally, our framework and its application can also help us better understand the psychology of fake news (Pennycook & Rand 2019, 2021). Why do people create, share, and believe fake news? These are basic questions whose answers are central to understanding the phenomenon of fake news in the modern world. Most notably, as we demonstrate through our analysis of the case of Jayson Blair and *The New York Times*, variation in the linguistic structure of fake news reflects the specific communicative goals of authors who consciously write fake news and the production circumstances in which fake news is produced. Appreciating the linguistic structure of fake news can also potentially help us understand why some fake news is more likely to be believed and to be shared, which may be especially important for combating the spread of fake news online.

1.3 Overview

Fake news is a long-standing problem, but it is receiving unprecedented attention today due to the rise of online news and social media, as well as growing distrust of the mainstream news media. Although fake news most commonly involves news texts, the study of the language of fake news has been limited, with researchers focusing more on the automated classification of true and false news than on explaining why the structure of real and fake news differs. It is therefore crucial to extend our understanding of the language of fake news, especially through the detailed analysis of real and fake news texts collected in a principled manner and grounded in linguistic theory.

Given this background, the goal of this Element is threefold. First, we introduce a new linguistic framework for the analysis of the language of fake news, focusing on understanding how the linguistic structure of fake news differs from real news, drawing especially on the distinction between misinformation and disinformation and the concept of register variation. Second, based on this framework, we conduct a detailed analysis of the language of fake news in the famous case of Jayson Blair and *The New York Times* to identify and explain systematic differences in the grammatical structure of his real and fake news.[1] Third, we consider how our results can help address the problem of fake news, including by informing research in natural language processing and psychology.

The remainder of this Element is organised as follows. In Section 2, we present a critical review of research on the language of fake news, before presenting our theoretical framework for the linguistic analysis of fake news, which directly addresses limitations with previous research. In Section 3, we review the case of Jayson Blair, including the background, the scandal, the investigation, and the aftermath. In Section 4, we describe the corpus of Jayson Blair's writings that we collected, which is the basis of this study. In Section 5, we present our main linguistic analysis, discussing a range of grammatical features that vary across Blair's real and fake news. We find that Blair's fake news is written in a less dense style than his real news and with less conviction. We then offer explanations for these findings based on specific factors that led Blair to write fake news. Finally, in Section 6, we consider the implications of our research for our understanding of fake news more generally.

2 Analysing the Language of Fake News

The language of fake news has received considerable attention in recent years, especially in natural language processing, where the focus has been on the development of machine learning systems for the automatic classification of real and fake news based on language content. In this section, we critically review recent research on the language of fake news, arguing that it has been limited by the definition of fake news as false news and the lack of control for other sources of linguistic variation. To address these issues, we propose a framework for the linguistic analysis of fake news that is grounded in theories of disinformation and register variation. This framework provides a basis for describing the linguistic differences between real and fake news and explaining why these differences exist.

---

[1] This study was approved by the University of Birmingham's ethics review panel. All data analysed are published and publicly available, including via in the online archives of *The New York Times*.

2.1 Defining Fake News

The first major challenge in the study of the language of fake news is to define fake news in such a way that instances of fake news texts can be identified and collected (Tandoc et al. 2018; Asr & Taboada 2019). There is, however, no simple or standard definition of fake news, which is better understood as the product of a range of practices that are related to the validity of information being shared by the news media. Researchers must therefore define the specific form of fake news they are interested in studying. Any coherent definition of fake news can be the starting point for meaningful empirical research, but researchers naturally tend to focus on certain types of fake news, depending both on the perceived societal importance of that type of fake news and the feasibility of collecting news texts of that type in a reliable and efficient manner – considerations that are often at odds with each other.

The vast majority of research on the language of fake news has been conducted in natural language processing and has focused on the development of tools for automatically distinguishing real and fake news (e.g. Conroy et al. 2015; Rubin et al. 2015; Shu et al. 2017; Asr & Taboada 2018; Bondielli & Marcelloni 2019; Oshikawa et al. 2020; Zhou & Zafarani 2020). In general, this research defines fake news as *false news* – untrue information disseminated by the news media. This has also been the definition that has been adopted in the very limited amount of linguistic research on this topic in discourse analysis (e.g. Igwebuike & Chimuanya 2021). Crucially, this definition of fake news is based on the underlying truth of the information being conveyed: to study fake news from this perspective, comparable corpora of *true* and *false* news must be compiled. For example, to develop a machine learning system capable of distinguishing between true and false news requires that many true and false news texts be collected so that the system can be trained and tested on this dataset.

A major advantage of this *veracity-based approach* to fake news research is that it allows fake news to be collected with relative ease. Most commonly this involves drawing on the work of fact-checking organisations and mainstream news media organisations that identify fake news, including both instances of fake news and sources of fake news (Asr & Taboada 2018). This information is then used as a basis for compiling a corpus of fake news texts. These texts most commonly include passages from news articles (e.g. Vlachos & Riedel 2014; Wang 2017), social media posts (e.g. Shu et al. 2017, 2020; Wang 2017; Santia & Williams 2018), and complete news articles (e.g. Rashkin et al. 2017; Horne & Adali 2017; Santia & Williams 2018; Castelo et al. 2019; Lin et al. 2019; Bonet-Jover et al. 2021). Alternatively, some studies have used crowdsourcing to conduct their own fact-checking, having people rate the veracity of social media posts (e.g. Mitra & Gilbert 2015) or news text (e.g. Pérez-Rosas et al. 2018). Crucially, these approaches not only make it possible for large collections of fake news to be compiled, but they maintain a certain degree of researcher objectivity, which is especially important in such a politicised domain. These collections of fake news are then generally contrasted with collections of true news, often collected from mainstream news media (e.g. Horne & Adali 2017; Rashkin et al. 2017; Pérez-Rosas et al. 2018; Castelo et al. 2019; Bonet-Jover et al. 2021).

In addition to the advantages of a veracity-based approach to the study of fake news, there are disadvantages. Most obviously, classifying news based on a true–false distinction inaccurately reduces the veracity of a news text down to a single binary variable. News texts, however, generally convey a large amount of information, some of which can be true and some of which can be false. Some fact-checking organisations and researchers have acknowledged this limitation, classifying fake news on a scale (e.g. Rashkin et al. 2017; Wang 2017), although such an approach still assumes veracity can be reduced to a single quantitative variable.

Analysing the language of fake news based on veracity also requires that someone judges what qualifies as true and false news. Relying on external fact-checking services is a common and convenient solution to this problem, but while it may appear to increase the objectivity of a study, by limiting the involvement of the researcher at this stage of data collection, it actually immediately politicises the study, linking the research directly to the policies of the fact-checking organisation. Furthermore, these policies are not always consistent or accessible, making it difficult for the validity and biases of such research to be assessed, even by the researchers themselves. Fact-checking organisations may even be invested in the dissemination of fake news.

Finally, the veracity-based approach risks taking focus away from the type of *deceptive* fake news that is generally of greatest societal concern. People are not primarily worried about *false news*, as inaccuracies might be unintentional or inconsequential, but about *deceptive news* that is intended to manipulate readers, especially for establishing forms of political, social, and economic control (Gelfert 2018). It is important to consider the full range of practices encompassed by the term *fake news*, but we must not lose sight of those forms of fake news that are most problematic, even if they are inevitably more difficult to study. We certainly should not assume that natural language processing systems trained to identify false news can be used to identify deceptive news with similar levels of accuracy, especially as deceptive news is presumably the type of fake news that is most difficult for humans to identify.

The distinction between *misinformation* and *disinformation* is especially relevant to this discussion, because it helps us better understand the range of phenomena referred to as *fake news,* and because it helps us better understand what types of fake news should be of greatest concern. Specifically, *misinformation* is defined as *false* information, whereas *disinformation* is defined as *deceptive* information (Stahl 2006; Rubin 2019). The distinction between *information* and *misinformation* is therefore grounded in the concept of *veracity*, defined independently of the knowledge or intent of the individual, whereas the distinction between *information* and *disinformation* is grounded in the concept of *deception*, defined relative to the knowledge and intent of the individual. Essentially, this terminology reflects the difference between a falsehood and a lie.

It is important to acknowledge that the distinction between misinformation and disinformation pre-dates the rise of modern concerns about online fake news, and traditionally disinformation was recognised as the greater problem (Fallis 2009). For example, Fetzer (2004: 231) wrote that

> The distinction between misinformation and disinformation becomes especially important in political, editorial, and advertising contexts, where sources may make deliberate efforts to mislead, deceive, or confuse an audience in order to promote their personal, religious, or ideological objectives.

Fetzer was not referring to fake news directly but highlighting how deception is of far greater concern than inaccuracy. Nevertheless, the veracity-based approach to the study of fake news, which dominates current research, tends to focus implicitly on misinformation, at least in part because it is far easier to identify instances of misinformation than disinformation in the news media, for example, by drawing on the work of fact-checking organisations. This approach allows researchers to work at the scale required to train and test modern machine learning systems, but it has effectively moved focus away from the central problem of fake news – deceptive and dishonest news practices.

In most discussions of misinformation and disinformation, misinformation is presented as the larger category, including both information that is accidentally false and information that is purposely false (Stahl 2006; Tandoc et al. 2018). In other words, disinformation is seen as a type of misinformation – purposeful misinformation. It is clearly necessary to draw a distinction between misinformation that qualifies and does not qualify as disinformation: people can inadvertently communicate falsehoods when they intend to share accurate information, and this should not be confused with lying. For example, a journalist might report false information obtained from a source, who the journalist believed was telling the truth. This qualifies as misinformation, but not disinformation, which only occurs when the journalist lies, reporting information they believe to be false.

It is wrong, however, to insist that all disinformation is misinformation, as people can also state the truth when they intend to deceive, if they are misinformed themselves. If Democritus, who believed the earth was flat, tried to convince his student that the earth was round (e.g. as part of a lesson), he would be deceiving his student, but inadvertently telling the truth. Situations such as these are presumably rare in journalism, although sustained disinformation campaigns would likely result in the production of some truthful disinformation over time. Perhaps a more common form of truthful disinformation in the news media is deception by omission, where the information contained in a news text is true, but important information is purposely excluded to manipulate the reader (Wenzel 2019). Most notably, this type of fake news would include selective and biased reporting. For example, the American news media has been criticised for reporting mass shootings differently, excluding relevant information, depending on the race of the shooter (Duxbury et al. 2018). Real news could even potentially contain purposeful falsehoods and contradictions, so as to allow true information to be communicated that could not otherwise be published openly (Strauss 1952).

The relationship between misinformation, disinformation, and fake news is illustrated in Figure 1, which shows the overlap between disinformation and misinformation along our two main dimensions of fake news: veracity and honesty (see also Tandoc et al. 2018). Prototypical real news is both honest and true: generally, the goal of journalists is to share information that is true *and*

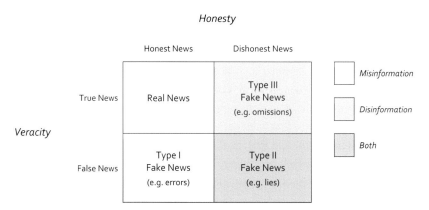

Figure 1 A typology of fake news

that they believe is true. However, there are three distinct ways news texts can diverge from this expectation, creating three broad categories of fake news. Type I Fake News is unintentionally false news, which occurs when journalists report information they believe to be true, but which is false. Type I Fake News therefore qualifies as misinformation but not disinformation. Alternatively, Type II Fake News is intentionally false news, which occurs when journalists purposely report information they believe to be false. Type II Fake News therefore qualifies as both misinformation and disinformation. Finally, Type III Fake News is news that is true but is nevertheless intended to deceive, including fake news by omission or selective reporting. Type III Fake News therefore qualifies as disinformation but not misinformation.

Our opinion is that research on fake news should primarily focus on disinformation, especially Type II Fake News – news that was intended to deceive its readership into believing information the journalist does not believe is true – as this is the type of fake news that we believe is of greatest societal concern. We also believe it is important not to conflate these different types of fake news: studies should either focus on one type of fake news, and compare it to real news, or distinguish between different types of fake news. In our analysis of the case of Jayson Blair and *The New York Times*, we therefore focus on comparing Type II Fake News, where Blair purposely published false information, to real news, where he purposely told the truth. Consequently, our framework and our study differ from most research on the language of fake news, which tends to focus on false news, effectively conflating Type I and Type II Fake News, obscuring the difference between misinformation and disinformation.

2.2 Language Variation and Fake News

The second major challenge in the study of the language of fake news is collecting comparable real and fake news texts for analysis. In general, research on the language of fake news, including fake news detection in natural language processing, is based on the comparison of patterns of language variation across texts that have been classified as real and fake. If this research is to identify actual differences between real and fake news, these texts must otherwise be as comparable as possible. We know, however, that there are many other factors that also naturally cause language variation across news texts, including variation in register, author, and dialect. Consequently, once fake news has been defined in a clear and practical manner, it is still necessary to identify real news for comparison that allows for these other sources of linguistic variation to be somehow controlled. The challenge is to build corpora that allow us to isolate variation between real and fake news.

Most importantly, to study the language of fake news, it is necessary to control for *register variation*, that is, variation based on communicative context and purpose (Biber & Conrad 2019). No matter how fake news is defined, we must contrast otherwise comparable registers of real and fake news. For example, if real news is collected from traditional newspapers and fake news is collected from blogs, it would be unclear if any observed differences in language use are related to differences between real and fake news or to differences between newspapers and blogs, which are associated with different communicative purposes and production circumstances, and which therefore show distinct patterns of grammatical variation (Biber 1988; Grieve et al. 2010). Specifically, blog writing is more informal than newspaper writing for a wide range of reasons, independent of its status as real or fake news. We would also likely find clear topical differences between these two registers of news, especially, for example, if fake news from fringe outlets online is compared to real news from the mainstream press.

This type of register imbalance is common in fake news datasets used in natural language processing. For example, the LIAR dataset (Wang 2017), which has been used in many studies (e.g. Shu et al. 2017; Aslam et al. 2021), consists of news statements that were scored for veracity by a major fact-checking organisation. The register of these statements, however, varies sub-stantially, including statements drawn from news reports, campaign speeches, and social media posts. No information is provided on how these registers were selected or whether the distribution of true and false statements is balanced across these categories, nor is register variation generally taken into account during analysis. Similarly, the Buzzfeed fake news dataset (Silverman et al. 2017), which has also been used in many studies (e.g. Shu et al. 2017; Mangal & Sharma 2021), was designed to allow for real and fake news to be compared between mainstream news outlets and extremist left- and right-wing websites. The dataset, however, is accompanied by descriptive statistics showing that data from mainstream news is rated at over 90 per cent true, whereas data from extremist websites is rated at around 50 per cent true. Fake news identification systems trained on such datasets may achieve high levels of accuracy, but this classification would likely be driven primarily by broad register differences between the texts selected to represent real and fake news as opposed to whether a text was real or fake, especially when fake news is largely concentrated in one register.

A related issue is that much research on the language of fake news tends to focus only on part of the news media landscape, especially non-traditional online sources, often associated with extreme political viewpoints, as the Buzzfeed fake news dataset clearly illustrates. This type of fake news is convenient to study because these are the sources that most fact-checking organisations target, and because labelling news from such sources as fake is less likely to be questioned, at least within the scientific community. There is no reason to doubt that fake news, including genuine disinformation, originates from these sources, but it is wrong to assume that these are the only sources of fake news, as our case of Jayson Blair and *The New York Times* and many of the examples we have considered thus far illustrate. In many ways, these are not even the most serious sources of fake news, because texts from non-traditional outlets are often obviously fake to a large proportion of the public, and because their status as potential fake news can often be inferred based entirely on source. Mainstream news media is generally excluded from fake news research, except as the source of true news comparison data. As a result, most fake news research does not generalise to fake news published by the mainstream news media, as fake news detection systems are trained to treat all mainstream news as real, even though this is the type of fake news that has the potential to be far more significant and difficult to detect.

In addition to register variation, it is also important to control other forms of linguistic variation when collecting comparable examples of real and fake news for analysis. For example, research in stylometry has shown that each author has their own style, with different sets of linguistic features distinguishing between the unique varieties of language used by individuals (Grieve 2007). Certain features used by one author to create real or fake news may therefore be different from other authors, introducing possible confounds in large-scale corpus-based research on fake news that does not attempt to control for individual differences.

Furthermore, we know the social background of authors more generally affects their writing style (Grieve 2016), so even taking large random samples of real and fake news written by many authors will not necessarily allow for sociolinguistic variation to be controlled. For example, it seems likely that when fake news is drawn from fringe online sources, and real news is drawn from the mainstream press, there will be clear social differences between the two sets of authors, especially in terms of education level and socioeconomic status, which are well-known correlates of dialect variation (Tagliamonte 2006). The apparent differences observed between real and fake news in previous studies therefore may also reflect differences in the social backgrounds of the authors being compared, as opposed to the status of the news as real or fake. For example, if authors of real news are primarily professional authors, while authors of fake news are primarily amateurs, we would expect broad differences in the language in which they write, regardless of whether or not they are telling the truth. Some research has begun to address these types of issues at least obliquely. For example, Potthast et al. (2017) found that hyper-partisan left- and right-wing news appears to share a style associated with the language of extremism. However, controlling for social variation in the authors of real and fake news is a topic that has received remarkably little attention in the literature, and represents another major limitation of current research on the language of fake news.

2.3 A Framework for the Linguistic Analysis of Fake News

To summarise, there are two key limitations with previous research on the language of fake news: researchers do not generally analyse the most problematic forms of fake news, focusing on misinformation as opposed to disinformation; and researchers do not generally control for other forms of linguistic variation, including variation in register, authorship, and dialect. These issues stem in part from reliance on fact-checking services for identifying fake news, as well as from the lack of a clear and meaningful definition of fake news. Consequently, researchers often miss the central problem of fake news or fail to isolate the distinction between real and fake news. To address these issues, we propose a framework for the linguistic analysis of fake news that is grounded in theories of disinformation and register variation.

We believe the language of fake news can best be understood as a form of register variation between information and disinformation in the news media. If we define fake news based on the communicative purpose of the journalist, as our focus on disinformation demands, the theories and methods of register analysis provide us with a basis for analysing the language of fake news in a meaningful way. Research on register variation has repeatedly shown that the use of a wide range of grammatical features varies systematically across contexts depending on their function (Halliday 1978; Chafe & Tannen 1987; Biber 1988; Biber & Conrad 2019). Because the communicative goals of people change across contexts, along with the inherent communicative affordances and constraints associated with those contexts, the structure of discourse varies systematically across contexts as well. Grammatical differences between registers are not arbitrary, but directly reflect how people vary their language for effective communication in different situations. As Halliday (1978: 31–2) writes, 'the notion of register is at once very simple and very powerful. It refers to the fact that the language we speak or write varies according to the type of situation'. For example, when people tell stories, they tend to use many past tense verbs, because they are recounting events that took place in the past (Biber 1988). These grammatical differences exist because the communicative needs of people vary across different contexts.

For this reason, we should expect that the language of real and fake news also varies systematically, if subtly, so long as real and fake news are defined based on the intent of the journalist, for instance, to inform or deceive. Register variation can therefore provide a basis for describing and explaining grammatical differences in the language of real and fake news, specifically between information and disinformation. This link between the concepts of disinformation and register variation is the basic theoretical insight that underlies our framework for the linguistic analysis of fake news.

Our framework draws most directly on the type of quantitative corpus-based register analysis developed by Douglas Biber and his colleagues, known as *multidimensional analysis* (Biber & Conrad 2019). Most notably, Biber (1988) presented an extensive analysis of linguistic variation across registers of written and spoken British English, identifying clear grammatical differences across registers, showing that these patterns derive from variation in communicative purpose and context. In total, six aggregated dimensions of register variation were extracted from the corpus based on a multivariate statistical analysis of sixty-seven grammatical features, whose relative frequencies were measured across each of the individual texts in the corpus. These dimensions were then interpreted functionally based on the most strongly associated features and texts. For example, the first dimension, which accounts for the largest amount of variance across the feature set, was interpreted as reflecting a distinction between more informational and more involved forms of communication. On the one hand, texts from registers like academic and newspaper writing were found to be relatively informational and formal, characterised by frequent use of features like nouns and noun modifiers, which are associated with a relatively dense style of communication. On the other hand, texts from registers like face-to-face and telephone conversations were found to be relatively involved and informal, characterised by frequent use of features like verbs, pronouns, and adverbs, which are associated with relatively casual and spontaneous discourse, and consequently lower levels of informational density. For example, conversations tend to contain many pronouns due to natural communicative constraints on the production of spontaneous speech, which greatly limit opportunities for individuals to compose complex noun phrases. Instead, individuals tend to repeatedly reference entities under discussion using pronouns, adding new information with each reference. Other dimensions of register variation identified in Biber (1988) are related to factors like narrativity, persuasion, and abstractness.

The extensive and interpretable set of grammatical features identified in Biber (1988) provides us with a basis for identifying meaningful differences between the linguistic structure of real and fake news that are directly related to variation in communicative function. These features have been validated through a long history of use for the empirical analysis of register variation in the English language, with features and clusters of features having been linked to a wide range of different communicative functions. These functional linguistic patterns can therefore help us understand the motivation for linguistic variation observed when comparing real and fake news. Notably, comparable feature sets have also been compiled for other languages, including Somali, Korean, and Tuvaluan (Biber 1995).

Drawing on insights from register analysis therefore allows us to address another basic limitation with current research on the language of fake news – reliance on relatively superficial feature sets, like the use of individual words and word sequences (i.e. n-grams), which are easy to count, but more difficult to explain, especially from a grammatical as opposed to a topical perspective. By describing differences between real and fake news based on an established set of grammatical features with clear functional relevance, we can overcome this limitation, and identify differences in the linguistic structure of real and fake news that are driven by differences in the communicative intent of journalists – to produce news texts that are intended to inform and news texts that are intended to deceive.

In addition to conceiving of variation between real and fake news as a form of register variation, our framework also acknowledges that there are other sources of linguistic variation in the news media, which might obscure differences between real and fake news if ignored. When compiling fake news corpora, it is especially important to control for other sources of register variation, as there are clear linguistic differences across news registers, reflecting variation in communicative purpose and context. For example, it would seem to be much easier for people to distinguish between different types of news texts – for example, newspaper articles and blog posts – than it is to identify whether the journalist is honest or dishonest. This is why fake news identification is such a challenging task. Controlling register variation can be achieved either by focusing on one news register or by factoring register variation into the analysis directly. Controlling register variation also helps control dialect variation, as the social background of people who produce different types of news inevitably differs, especially in terms of education and class. For example, it seems likely that writers at mainstream newspapers are generally more highly educated than social media posters. Such differences will have clear linguistic consequences that must somehow be controlled in any rigorous study of fake news. Finally, it is important to control directly for authorship to account for individual differences of style, ideally by considering the language of one or more authors who are known to have produced both real and fake news.

Overall, by treating disinformation in the news media as a form of register variation, by drawing on a rich and interpretable grammatical feature set, and by controlling for other important sources of linguistic variation, we believe it is possible not only to identify actual differences in the language of real and fake news but to offer explanations for why these differences exist, based on variation in the communicative goals of journalists, as well as the production circumstances in which they write. In this way, we address a final limitation with current research on the language of fake news – the lack of any underlying theory for why real and fake news should differ or any explanation for why observed differences in the language of real and fake news exist. Providing the basis for truly understanding the language of fake news is the primary goal of this Element. Furthermore, our framework should be of direct value to work on fake news detection in natural language processing, because it provides a theoretical basis for detection, which can help improve the performance of these tools, especially in the most challenging cases, and because it provides justification for the application of these tools in real-world settings.

Finally, it is important to acknowledge that while there is good reason to assume systematic linguistic differences exist between news media texts that are intended to inform and deceive, this assumption does not extend to news media texts that are true and false. This is because misinformation may be shared without the knowledge of the journalist, precluding the possibility that differences in language structure arise from differences in communicative purpose. In fact, from this perspective, it is unclear why we should expect systematic linguistic differences between true and false news to exist at all, further calling into question standard approaches to the analysis of fake news based on fact-checked data. Unfortunately, the study of disinformation is more challenging than the study of misinformation, as it requires knowledge of the intent of an author, which is often inaccessible to researchers. Nevertheless, as the case of Jayson Blair and *The New York Times* demonstrates, such cases do exist and can be identified if we take the time to review the history of the news media. In the next three chapters, we therefore focus on this one important case of fake news, not only to demonstrate the application of our framework but to begin to truly understand the language of fake news.

3 Jayson Blair and *the New York Times*

The New York Times was established in 1851 and has long been regarded as one of the most important newspapers in the world – for many the newspaper of record in the United States. *The Times* has won over 130 Pulitzer Prizes, more than any other newspaper, and is ranked in the top 20 newspapers in the world and the top 3 newspapers in the United States by circulation (Cision Media Research 2019). Despite its reputation, like most newspapers, *The Times* has been subject to criticism for the honesty and accuracy of its reporting. In this Element, we focus on one such case, the Jayson Blair scandal, a famous example of fake news at *The Times* from the early 2000s. This event was described by a large number of news reports (Barry et al. 2003; Hernandez 2003a, 2003b; Kelley 2003; Kurtz 2003a, 2003b, 2003c, 2003d, 2003e; Leo 2003; Magden 2003; New York Times 2003a, 2003b; Newsweek 2003; Steinberg 2003a, 2003b, 2003c, 2003d; Woo 2003; Keller 2005; Barron 2006; Calame 2006; Scocca 2006), and books (Blair 2004; Mnookin 2004) from this time, as well as limited academic research (Hindman 2005; Patterson & Urbanski 2006). In this section, we introduce this case by presenting a synthesis of these accounts.

Jayson Blair was born in 1976, the son of a federal official and a schoolteacher. He grew up outside Washington D.C., in Centreville, Virginia. As a student, he worked at *The Sentinel,* the student newspaper at Centreville High School, and *The Diamondback*, the student newspaper at the University of Maryland, where he pursued a degree in journalism. During his studies, he interned at *The Boston Globe, The Washington Post,* and, for ten weeks in the summer of 1998, *The New York Times.* His work during this final internship, over which time he wrote nineteen articles, led to Blair being offered a position at *The Times* before he graduated. He accepted in June 1999, when he was only twenty-three years old, joining the newspaper's Police Bureau, instead of finishing his studies.

Over the next four years at *The Times*, Blair published more than 600 articles on a wide range of topics. His career progressed quickly. Soon after joining the newspaper, in November 1999, he was promoted from intern to intermediate reporter, moving to the Metropolitan Desk, where he gained a reputation for being highly productive and charismatic. In January 2001, Blair was promoted again to full-time reporter. After a brief stint on the Sports Desk, he was moved to the prestigious National Desk in October 2002 by the newspaper's two top editors, Howell Raines and Gerald Boyd. Along with several other reporters, Blair was tasked with covering the D.C. Sniper Attacks, the biggest news story in the nation, which was unfolding near his hometown. Blair appeared to make the most of this opportunity over the next year, including publishing front-page features. In recognition of his success, Blair was assigned to lead coverage on the trial, following the arrest of John Muhammad and his teenage accomplice Lee Malvo. In March 2003, Blair was also assigned to report on the Iraq War from a domestic perspective as part of the newspaper's *Nation at War* series. Most notably, he covered the story of Jessica Lynch, an American soldier who had famously been captured and then rescued in Iraq. In recognition of his accomplishments, his editors at *The Times* were considering promoting him once again in April 2003, but these would be among the last articles Blair would write.

Despite his rapid rise, Blair's reporting had long been the subject of concern for some of his editors at *The Times*. Jonathan Landman, who became Blair's editor at the Metropolitan Desk not long after he joined the newspaper, appears to have been Blair's most vocal critic. In late 2000, Joseph Lelyveld, the executive editor at *The Times,* expressed concern over the number of errors being published by the newspaper, prompting Landman to conduct a review of corrections coming from his staff at the Metropolitan Desk. Although Landman had misgivings when Blair was promoted to full-time reporter in January 2001, he did not oppose the promotion. His concerns grew, however, not long after the September 11 attacks, when Blair published an article that was found to contain many factual errors. Blair claimed he was distracted by the loss of his cousin in the attack on the Pentagon. He also wrote a letter of apology to Landman. Nevertheless, in January 2002, Landman submitted a highly critical evaluation of Blair, highlighting his extremely high correction rate, resulting in a two-week leave of absence. By April 2002, Landman had become so concerned that he emailed senior colleagues recommending they terminate Blair's contract. Instead Blair was asked to take another leave of absence. When he returned, Landman took it upon himself to monitor Blair's output, leading to a reduction both in his publication and correction rates. Blair, however, soon left the Metropolitan Desk, and Landman's supervision, eventually being assigned to the National Desk, where he covered the D.C. Sniper Attacks and the Iraq War. The increased attention garnered by these new national assignments would soon lead directly to Blair's undoing.

Although they made the front page, Blair's articles on the D.C. Sniper were highly controversial, attracting criticism from both inside and outside *The Times*. For example, in his first front-page article, citing anonymous sources, Blair implied that tensions between law enforcement agencies had led to the interrogation of Muhammad being cut short just as he was about to confess, a claim that was vehemently denied by government officials. In another front-page article, once again citing anonymous sources, Blair reported that Malvo had been the primary shooter, leading to the prosecutor from Virginia calling a press conference to publicly reject his claims. These issues led to renewed scrutiny of Blair's work, but Blair continued reporting, transitioning to domestic coverage of the Iraq War starting in March 2003. This time he attracted criticism from the *San Antonio Express-News*. Another young reporter, Macarena Hernandez, who had interned with Blair at *The Times* five years earlier, noticed that a front-page article by Blair published on 26 April

('Family Waits, Now Alone, for a Missing Soldier') contained very similar details as her front-page article published by *The Express-News* on 18 April ('Texas soldier; Valley mom awaits news of MIA son'), which recounted an interview with the family of this same missing soldier. In response, the editor of *The Express-News,* Robert Rivard, sent an email to Blair's editors at *The Times* on 29 April alleging plagiarism.

The Times immediately started an investigation, but before Raines and Boyd could assemble their team, *The Washington Post* broke the story. A few days after Blair's article was published, Hernandez had returned to Los Fresnos. The family's son had been discovered dead in Iraq. There she happened to discuss Blair with a reporter from *The Post,* who had also noticed similarities between the two articles. Later that day, Howard Kurtz, the media reporter for *The Post,* contacted Hernandez for comment. Kurtz published his first report on the scandal on 30 April ('New York Times Story Gives Texas Paper Sense of Deja Vu'), quoting both Hernandez and Rivard, presumably greatly increasing pressure on *The Times* and Blair, who would resign the next day.

Blair's resignation was announced by *The Times* in an 'Editors' Note' published on 2 May, which also acknowledged plagiarism in his article from 26 April. *The Times* also published a second short news article reporting on the case written by Jacques Steinberg ('Times Reporter Resigns After Questions on Article'). The report quotes Raines apologising to the readers of *The Times*, as well as the family of the dead soldier, for 'a grave breach of its journalistic standards', assuring that a full investigation was underway:

> We continue to examine the circumstances of Mr. Blair's reporting about the Texas family. In also reviewing other journalistic work he has done for The Times, we will do what is necessary to be sure the record is kept straight.

The reports also discussed the plagiarised article, highlighting Blair's transgressions. For example, although the article bore a Los Fresnos dateline and reported details about the family's home, implying that it was written on site, the family claimed that they had never been interviewed by Blair.

A full investigation of the seventy-three articles published by Blair after joining the national desk in late October 2002 was completed over the next two weeks. The investigation started officially on 5 May, once Dan Barry, a Pulitzer Prize winner who had been with *The Times* since 1993, agreed to lead the investigation. In addition to Steinberg, he was joined by David Barstow, Jonathan Glater, and Adam Liptak, who were selected by Raines and Boyd. The reporters immediately demanded independence from the editors, whose management style and relationship with Blair were very much in question. This was a controversial decision, as Boyd in particular was legally obliged to read all reports published by *The Times*. Fortunately, Al Siegal, the assistant managing editor in charge of corrections, who had worked at the newspaper for decades, agreed to oversee the investigation in their place. The investigation culminated with the publication of three articles on 11 May, approved by Siegal, without having been seen by the two top editors at *The Times,* nor the publisher, Arthur Sulzberger Jr, whose family had run the newspaper since 1896. Sulzberger was quoted, however, by the investigation as saying that the scandal was 'a huge black eye' for the newspaper.

The first article was an 'Editors' Note' (totalling approximately 400 words) acknowledging the extent of the incident, Blair's resignation, and the investigation, as well as expressing the newspaper's regret for not identifying Blair's deceptions sooner. The article claimed that the investigation had found that thirty-seven articles authored by Jayson Blair and published by *The Times* since October 2002 had been plagiarised or fabricated, including the article from 26 April. The article explained the investigation focused on Blair's work over this period because this is when he was moved to the National Desk and consequently given greater freedom – and hence greater opportunity for impropriety. Earlier articles were therefore only being spot-checked. The article also outlined the steps taken by the investigative team, who conducted interviews and examined Blair's records, including his phone logs and expense reports.

The second article was a report (totalling approximately 7,000 words) written by the five reporters who had led the investigation ('Times Reporter Who Resigned Leaves Long Trail of Deception'). This article focused especially on describing Blair's activities since he had joined the national desk but also contained an extended discussion of Blair's history at *The Times*. Notably, the report opened with a frank admission:

> A staff reporter for The New York Times committed frequent acts of journalistic fraud while covering significant news events in recent months, an investigation by Times journalists has found. The widespread fabrication and plagiarism represent a profound betrayal of trust and a low point in the 152-year history of the newspaper.

The report then went on to directly acknowledge the extent of Blair's deception and the range of ways in which he breached the basic ethical standards of journalism.

> The reporter, Jayson Blair, 27, misled readers and Times colleagues with dispatches that purported to be from Maryland, Texas and other states, when often he was far away, in New York. He fabricated comments. He concocted scenes. He lifted material from other newspapers and wire services. He selected details from photographs to create the impression he had been somewhere or seen someone, when he had not.

Based on over 150 interviews with Blair's colleagues and alleged sources, and the examination of a range of business records and emails, as well as reports from other news agencies, the investigation concluded that Blair was responsible for 'systematic fraud' over his career at *The Times.* He had even lied about losing a cousin in the attack on the Pentagon. The report also discussed the circumstances that gave rise to the scandal, primarily identifying issues with Blair's character, as well as failures by his editors to communicate their concerns about Blair, and a lack of complaints from people who were misrepresented in Blair's articles.

Most notably, the report found that Blair rarely left New York, including when he was assigned to cover the D.C. Sniper Crisis or to meet families from across the US who had lost sons and daughters in the Iraq War. For example, the report detailed issues with an article from 27 March ('Relatives of Missing Soldiers Dread Hearing Worse News'), which recounted an interview conducted by Blair with Jessica Lynch's father in Palestine, West Virginia. Blair described how her father became overwhelmed by emotion as they discussed his missing daughter on the porch of their family home, overlooking tobacco fields and cow pastures. Blair also reported that her brother was in the National Guard, continuing a long tradition of military service in her family. None of this was true. The family home did not overlook such a landscape, her brother was in the Army, and the family did not have a long military record. Blair had never even travelled to West Virginia, despite filing five articles about the Lynch family from the state. Instead, his email and phone records suggested he was in New York all along.

The third article was a report (totalling approximately 7,000 words) presenting the results of the investigation ('Witnesses and Documents Unveil Deceptions in a Reporter's Work'). The report focused on thirty-six articles published since late October 2002, excluding the article from 26 April that precipitated the investigation. For each of the thirty-six articles, the date and title were provided as well as a list of inaccuracies, classified into five categories: Denied Reports, Factual Errors, Whereabouts, Plagiarism, and Other Issues (e.g. misattributions, breaches of confidence). In addition, the report listed three articles published before this period in which errors had been identified. This final report provides a detailed record of how the credibility of one of the most important newspapers in the world was tarnished by the acts of one reporter who published a series of articles which today would be considered blatant examples of fake news.

Unsurprisingly, the case also received considerable attention from other news organisations. Reporting by Kurtz, who had broken the story for *The Washington Post,* was especially influential. On 2 May, the same day *The Times* publicly acknowledged that Blair had plagiarised *The Express-News*, Kurtz revealed that Blair had never graduated from the University of Maryland, a fact that was apparently unknown to many of his colleagues at *The Times*. Then, on 10 May, a day before *The Times* published the results of its investigation, Kurtz reported that Blair had also fabricated news in 1999 while working as an intern at *The Boston Globe*. Crucially, this was the first evidence that Blair's lies were more widespread. Next, on 12 May, Kurtz reported on the reaction of the news media to the scandal, highlighting questions about race and affirmative action – whether Blair had been given preferential treatment for being African American.

Blair had first come to *The Times* as part of a programme intended to diversify the newsroom, along with three other interns, who notably all went on to have very successful careers in journalism. While Macarena Hernandez would move back to San Antonio, Winnie Hu and Edward Wong still write for *The Times*. Hu works at the Metropolitan Desk, and Wong, who reported from Baghdad between 2004 and 2007, is now a diplomatic correspondent in Washington.

In their reports, *The Times* had only addressed the issue of race briefly. Most notably, Boyd, who had led the committee that promoted Blair to full-time reporter, was quoted as saying that race was not an issue:

> To say now that his promotion was about diversity in my view doesn't begin to capture what was going on. He was a young, promising reporter who had done a job that warranted promotion.

Boyd's relationship with Blair, however, was part of what was being questioned by the news media, especially as Boyd was also African American – as managing editor, the most highly ranked African American in the history of the newspaper at that time. For example, Kurtz quoted John Leo, a columnist from *U.S. News and World Report,* who had *once* worked at *The Times*:

> [W]ould this young African-American's meteoric rise to staff reporter be likely for a white reporter with comparable credentials? It appears as though the Times knew early on that hiring Blair was a dicey proposition.

Similarly, Kurtz quoted an editorial by *Newsweek,* which claimed that this was also the view of many of his colleagues at *The Times*:

> Internally, reporters had wondered for years whether Blair was given so many chances – and whether he was hired in the first place – because he was a promising, if unpolished, black reporter on a staff that continues to be, like most newsrooms in the country, mostly white.

Race was also addressed by senior columnists at *The Times* in the coming days, including William Safire, who published an ambiguous editorial titled 'A Huge Black Eye', and Bob Herbert, who wrote unambiguously that 'the race issue in this case is as bogus as some of Jayson Blair's reporting'.

The *Newsweek* article also directly questioned why the actions of Raines and Boyd had not been subjected to greater scrutiny by the investigation, especially given rumours that they had lost the confidence of much of the newsroom well before the scandal had come to light. *Newsweek* implied that Blair's 'close mentoring relationship' with Boyd, including frequent cigarette breaks together, was part of the problem, and that moving a young reporter like Blair to the National Desk was only necessary because Raines and Boyd had driven away so many senior reporters. Part of their strategy was to assign large numbers of reporters to major stories, thereby creating an aggressive environment where journalists not only competed for news but the support of their editors. The situation erupted at a staff-wide meeting on 14 May, a few days after the reports were published. Raines took responsibility for the breakdown in journalistic oversight, but staff apparently used the opportunity to attack Raines for how he ran the newsroom. Only a month later, Raines and Boyd would be forced to resign. Bill Keller would take over as executive editor in July 2003, while Raines and Boyd would go on to write books recounting their tenure at *The Times*. Boyd died of lung cancer in 2006. At his funeral, George Curry, who had worked with Boyd at *The St. Louis Post-Dispatch,* said that 'Gerald was a victim of Jayson Blair, not his protector'.

Blair also went on to publish a book in 2004 entitled *Burning down my Master's House: My Life at The New York Times.* The book opens with a clear admission of guilt:

> I lied and I lied – and then I lied some more. I lied about where I'd been, I lied about where I'd found information, I lied about how I wrote the story. And these were no everyday little white lies – they were complete fantasies, embellished down to the tiniest detail.

In addition, Blair acknowledged the investigation conducted by *The Times*, offering further support of its validity. He did, however, offer a somewhat different picture of why he lied. As opposed to the initial reports, which focused on Blair's character, Blair claimed that he fabricated news primarily because of the pressure placed on him by his editors at *The New York Times*, as well as his own personal drive for success. As the title of the book suggests, Blair also directly addressed the issues around race and affirmative action at *The Times*.

Another contributing factor cited by Blair was his struggles with manic depression, which he claimed were greatly exacerbated by the dysfunctional state of the newsroom. Remarkably, this angle was never acknowledged by *The Times* in their early reporting on the case. Blair's issues were first reported by *Newsweek* on 19 May, whose reporters had conducted an interview with Blair. Blair was quoted as saying (Magden 2003):

> I can't say anything other than the fact that I feel a range of emotions, including guilt, shame, sadness, betrayal, freedom and appreciation for those who have stood by me, been tough on me and have taken the time to understand that there is a deeper story and not to believe everything they read in the newspapers.

It is notable that the first acknowledgement of Blair's depression we can find in *The Times* was in a scathing review of Blair's book (Shafer 2004), published almost a year after the scandal first hit the press. The review opened with the question 'Should you believe anything written by a serial liar?' For *The Times,* the answer was clear, including for the role of Blair's struggle with depression, which the article dismissed as an excuse:

> Blair rappels down Mount Excuse, blaming everybody but himself for his offenses. He continually cites his manic-depressive illness to explain his behavior. For instance, he claims to have composed the Times story that got him busted – a Page 1 piece about the mother of an Iraq war fatality, which plagiarized The San Antonio Express-News – over a blackout weekend in his apartment that he can barely recall.

Although *the Times* did not accept depression as an excuse for deception, it was very much in their best interest to cast doubt on any claim that Blair's actions resulted from the pressures of the newsroom.

The scandal did lead to some institutional change at *The Times*. Two new editorships were created. Siegal became the first standards editor, a position that exists to this day, whose purpose is to ensure that the ethical standards of the newspaper are met. As standards editor, Siegal also led a committee that examined the culture of the newsroom, producing two reports that made recommendations about how to increase reader confidence in *The Times*. The first report, published in 2003, recommended the establishment of a public editor, an ombudsperson to scrutinise the newspaper externally. Keller approved the post in one of his first acts as executive editor. Notably, the post was terminated by Sulzberger in 2017 (Spayd 2017) in the wake of Trump's election, drawing widespread criticism, given growing dissatisfaction with mainstream news at the time, as well as broader concerns about fake news (Calderone 2017). Sulzberger claimed there was no longer any need for an ombudsperson because readers themselves had 'come together' through social media to 'collectively serve as a modern watchdog'. Whether he expected readers to detect the types of fabrications perpetrated by Blair that had led to the establishment of the position in the first place is unclear.

Finally, the second Siegal report, published in 2005, recommended addressing a range of issues in the *New York Times* newsroom, including through fact checking, correction tracking, and limiting the use of anonymous sources. Following its publication, Keller published a message to his staff. Notably, he did not mention Blair by name, only acknowledging that the Siegal reports were 'inspired by a specific wound to our reputation'. Instead, he reflected more generally on how the types of changes being proposed might address the larger issues that were facing the news media at that time:

> Will these reforms, by themselves, reverse the decline of public trust in news organizations? Of course not. There are too many factors beyond our control: the clamor of partisan critics on the right and left, who want journalism that conforms to their beliefs; the shouting heads who have made denunciation of the serious press part of their commercial shtick; the confusion, in this world of paid propaganda, blogged argument, tabloid gossip and cable shouting matches, about who is a journalist, and whether anyone can be trusted.

This quote is still relevant today, although Keller failed to acknowledge that traditional print media was in the process of being overtaken by online news, a shift, now complete, that was likely putting far greater pressure on the newspaper than any of Blair's actions. This was the news media landscape from which Blair emerged. Blair was a young, intelligent, and ambitious reporter who exploited growing uncertainty about the future of the news media, fabricating news for his own reputational and material benefit at the expense of an informed populace. His lies were not spread via social media, but he took advantage of new opportunities afforded by the Internet and digital communication to fabricate news and evade his editors.

4 Corpus

The case of Jayson Blair and *The New York Times* has been the subject of some academic research, mostly in communication and media studies (Hindman 2005; Patterson & Urbanski 2006; Spurlock 2016). To the best of our knowledge, Blair's writings have never been the focus of research in linguistics or natural language processing. The Jayson Blair case therefore provides us with a new and unique opportunity to conduct a highly controlled comparison of the language of real and fake news (Type II Fake News), allowing for many of the issues that have undermined previous research on fake news to be addressed, including controlling for variation in register, dialect, authorship, news outlet, topic, and political bias. Most critically, this case allows us to study the language of fake news in the writings of one journalist based on deception as opposed to veracity, given the detailed investigation conducted by *The Times,* as well as Blair's own admissions. In this section, we introduce our corpus.

To build a corpus of Blair's real and fake news, we collected the seventy-three articles that were published by Blair between 25 October 2002 and 29 April 2003 after he joined the National Desk, although not all were written for the National Desk. These are the seventy-three articles that were the subject of the main investigation conducted by the *Times,* as presented in the 11 May reports. Although we know that Blair had written fake news before this date, we restrict our analysis to articles published over these six months because this was the period covered by the comprehensive review conducted by *The Times.* Before this date, articles were only spot-checked, making it especially difficult to collect examples of real news from outside this period with confidence. The investigation explicitly identified thirty-seven fake articles (Type II Fake News) that Blair had written over this period, including the 26 April article on the Texas family who had lost their son in Iraq. In addition to being listed in the 11 May reports, each of these articles is marked in the online archive of *The Times,* as well as the Nexis newspaper database.

Notably, Blair's real articles were never listed explicitly in any official documentation from *The Times*: they are simply the thirty-six articles from the period under investigation that were not listed in the 11 May reports. To check these counts, we conducted an independent review of all articles published over this period listing Jayson Blair in the byline, using both the online archive of *The Times* and the Nexis news database. In addition to the thirty-seven fake news articles identified in the 11 May reports, all of which are accessible and have corrections appended in both archives, we found thirty-six additional articles authored by Blair over this period, giving the expected seventy-three articles. Two of the thirty-six real news articles did have corrections appended, but they are minor, relating to misspellings, which were presumably unintentional. Given our definition of fake news, which focuses on intentional deception, we therefore retained these two articles as examples of real news. However, we removed one fake article and three real articles from the corpus that were co-authored to focus our analysis on variation in Blair's writing style. Alternatively, we retained three fake articles and two real articles authored by Blair that were listed (on Nexis) as having contributions from other journalists because these articles were authored by Blair, only drawing on information provided by others. After all, we know that much of his fake news was drawing on information provided by other journalists as well, just without their consent.

We then removed titles, bylines, captions, and all other text that was outside the body of the main article. Finally, because our analysis is based on the relative frequency of grammatical forms, we removed short articles from our corpus. The relative frequencies of grammatical forms are only useful when the texts under analysis are long enough to provide us with enough word tokens for rates of use to be estimated meaningfully. We therefore excluded articles under 300 words, a common cut-off in authorship analysis (Grieve 2007), resulting in five additional real articles being excluded from our corpus. Following this process, our final corpus contains sixty-four articles, including thirty-six fake articles and twenty-eight real articles, all single authored by Blair between 25 October 2002 and 29 April 2003. The articles range in length from 321 to 1,825 words with a mean of 980 words for fake articles (with a standard deviation of 431 words) and a mean of 748 words for real articles (with a standard deviation of 315 words), showing an immediate difference between the form of these two types of texts. The total corpus contains 56,982 words, including 35,262 words of fake news and 21,720 words of real news. The vast majority of these articles were published by the National Desk, but there were also a handful of articles published over this period by the Metropolitan and Sports Desks, as well as in the *Week in Review* section. The final corpus is described in Table 1, which lists all sixty-four articles in the final corpus.

Before presenting the results of our analysis of this corpus, it is important to consider its composition. In Figure 2, we visualise our corpus from various perspectives, including based on topic, status as fake news, and time. The first panel presents a mosaic plot visualising the proportion of real and fake news by topic, ordered by proportion of fake news. Over this period Blair was primarily tasked with covering the D.C. Sniper Attacks, where about half his articles in our corpus were faked (46 per cent), and the effects of the Iraq War on the home front, where all his articles in our corpus were faked. Articles on the Sniper Attacks are especially common over this period, accounting for forty-six of the sixty-four texts in our corpus (72 per cent). In addition, Blair wrote a small number of articles on sports and other topics, including crime and death.

The second panel presents the number of fake and real news publications over time. We can see that Blair tended to publish articles in bursts, with three main clusters visible. Aside from a busy period in early November 2002, we can also see that his articles became both more frequent and more likely to be fabricated over time, especially in late March and early April 2003 before he was forced to resign. In addition, we can see that once Blair started publishing fake articles, whenever he published more than one article on the same day, at least one of these articles were faked. Crucially, however, we can see that overall he published real and fake articles over the same period, for example, with at least one real and one fake news article published in each of the seven months represented by this corpus.

The third panel combines this information and presents the distribution of publications by topic and news type over time, with larger circles representing multiple articles on the same topic and of the same type being published on the same day. The most important observation is that Blair's reporting on the Sniper Attacks became less reliable over time; when he switched to focusing on

Table 1 The Jayson Blair fake news corpus

Type	Index	Date	Desk	Headline	Topic	Words
Fake	F01	2002–10–30	National	U.S. Sniper Case Seen as a Barrier to a Confession	Sniper	1,310
	F02	2002–11–02	National	Sniper Suspects Linked To Yet Another Shooting	Sniper	870
	F03	2002–11–10	National	Officials Link Most Killings To Teenager	Sniper	609
	F04	2002–11–11	National	Statements by Teenager May Muddy Sniper Case	Sniper	992
	F05	2002–11–23	Sports	Attendance Requirement Leaves Colleges Sweating	Sport	1,478
	F06	2002–11–27	National	Questions Over the Reward For Tips in the Sniper Case	Sniper	602
	F07	2002–12–13	National	Laura Bush Visits the Youngest Sniper Victim	Sniper	367
	F08	2002–12–17	National	Sniper Case Will Be First Test of Virginia Antiterrorism Law	Sniper	672
	F09	2002–12–17	National	Man Who Shot Priest in an Abuse Case Wins Acquittal	Sniper	715
	F10	2002–12–18	National	Acquittal in Shooting Of Priest Splits a City	Crime	790
	F11	2002–12–22	National	Teenager's Role Tangles Case Against Older Sniper Suspect	Sniper	1,558
	F12	2003–01–02	National	Execution Opponent Joins Sniper Case	Sniper	800
	F13	2003–01–06	National	Prints Reportedly Tie Sniper Suspect to Killing	Sniper	631
	F14	2003–01–18	National	Like Sniper Case, Hearing for Youth Is Out of the Ordinary	Sniper	1,030
	F15	2003–01–19	National	In Absence of Parents, A Voice for the Accused	Sniper	1,200
	F16	2003–01–25	National	Gun Tests Said to Bolster Sniper Case Against Two	Sniper	441
	F17	2003–02–10	National	Peace and Answers Eluding Victims of the Sniper Attacks	Sniper	1,825

ID	Date	Scope	Title	Category	Count
F18	2003-03-03	National	Making Sniper Suspect Talk Puts Detective in Spotlight	Sniper	854
F19	2003-03-04	National	Judge in Sniper Case Bars Cameras From Trial	Sniper	523
F20	2003-03-08	National	Sniper Suspect Is Disciplined for Cell Graffiti	Sniper	459
F21	2003-03-22	National	Bearing the Worst News, Then Helping the Healing	War	694
F22	2003-03-22	National	Chief in Sniper Case Considers a Job Change	Sniper	980
F23	2003-03-25	National	Watching, and Praying, As a Son's Fate Unfolds	War	1,722
F24	2003-03-27	National	Relatives of Missing Soldiers Dread Hearing Worse News	War	1,497
F25	2003-03-31	National	For Families of the Dead, A Fateful Knock on the Door (Note: *with contributions from Monica Davey*)	War	1,301
F26	2003-04-01	National	The Last Stop on the Journey Home	War	941
F27	2003-04-04	National	Freed Soldier Is in Better Condition Than First Thought, Father Says	War	938
F28	2003-04-05	National	Tapes Hint at Possible Flaws In Sniper Suspect Confession	Sniper	1,110
F29	2003-04-05	National	Gifts and Offers for Book Deals Arrive at Rescued Private's House as She Has Surgery (Note: *with contributions from Mark Landler*)	War	694
F30	2003-04-06	National	Family Begins Trip to Rejoin Freed Soldier	War	354
F31	2003-04-07	National	For One Pastor, the War Hits Home	War	1,104
F32	2003-04-13	National	Former P.O.W. Returns Home For Treatment at Army Hospital	War	472
F33	2003-04-15	National	A Couple Separated by War While United in Their Fears (Note: *with contributions from Michael Wilson*)	War	1,819
F34	2003-04-19	National	In Military Wards, Questions and Fears From the Wounded	War	1,698

Table 1 (cont.)

Type	Index	Date	Desk	Headline	Topic	Words
	F35	2003–04–26	National	Family Waits, Now Alone, for a Missing Soldier	War	1,424
	F36	2003–04–29	National	Detective Says Sniper Suspect Was Interrogated After He Requested Lawyer	Sniper	788
Real	R01	2002–10–25	National	A Moment of Happy Fame for a Town	Sniper	550
	R02	2002–10–25	National	After Three Weeks of Tension, Face of Inquiry Wears a Smile	Sniper	894
	R03	2002–10–26	National	Checkpoints; The 2 Suspects Were Stopped By the Police Several Times (Note: *with contributions from Al Baker*)	Sniper	770
	R04	2002–10–27	National	Drivers Attend a Fallen Colleague's Funeral to Pay Respects and to Move On	Sniper	690
	R05	2002–10–28	National	Slaying Of Woman in Sniper Attacks Laid to Teenager (Note: *with contributions from Eric Lichtblau*)	Sniper	1,476
	R06	2002–10–31	National	Prosecutor Says U.S. Involvement Did Not Block Sniper Confession	Sniper	728
	R07	2002–11–05	National	Young Sniping Suspect Ordered Held Till Trial	Sniper	565
	R08	2002–11–06	National	Defendant in Sniper Case Ordered Held Without Bail	Sniper	776
	R09	2002–11–07	National	Prosecutor in Virginia Files Charges in Sniper Shootings	Sniper	702
	R10	2002–11–09	National	As Sniper Suspects Go to Court, State Cites New Evidence Against One	Sniper	1,186

ID	Date	Section	Title	Category	Number
R11	2002–11–12	National	Young Sniper Suspect Was Confused on Rights, Lawyers Say	Sniper	731
R12	2002–11–14	National	Older Sniper Suspect's Lawyers Consider a Change of Venue	Sniper	436
R13	2002–11–20	National	Sniper Defendant's Bid for Experts Is Rejected	Sniper	678
R14	2002–11–21	National	Mother of Sniper Suspect Is Ordered Back to Jamaica	Sniper	818
R15	2002–12–24	Metro	Harvey B. Scribner, New York Schools Chancellor in a Turbulent Era, Dies at 88	Death	1,506

(Note: corrections for spelling errors)

ID	Date	Section	Title	Category	Number
R16	2002–12–31	National	Defense in Sniper Case Wins Access to Police Interviews	Sniper	875
R17	2003–01–07	National	Mother Used Sniper Suspect As Collateral, Report Says	Sniper	533
R18	2003–01–15	National	Hearing Starts for Teenager in Virginia Sniper Case	Sniper	1,249
R19	2003–01–16	National	Teenager Held in Sniper Case Will Be Tried as Adult	Sniper	1,166
R20	2003–01–22	National	Virginia Indicts Young Sniper Suspect on Murder Charges	Sniper	645
R21	2003–02–27	National	Sniper Case Defense Lawyers Seek Voiding of a Confession	Sniper	738
R22	2003–03–03	Sports	After Ward Steps Down, There Are Still Concerns	Sport	707
R23	2003–03–13	National	Lawyers Plan Jury Challenge In Sniper Case	Sniper	321
R24	2003–03–15	Sports	New Owners but the Same City for the Sabres	Sport	403
R25	2003–03–21	National	Police Chief In Sniper Hunt May Not Profit From Memoir	Sniper	420
R26	2003–03–22	National	Motion Contends Sniper Defendant Killed 2	Sniper	375
R27	2003–04–07	National	Report Describes Sniper Suspect's Defiance Under Questioning	Sniper	535
R28	2003–04–12	National	Lawyers for Sniper Suspect Raise Issue of Chemical Exposure	Sniper	459

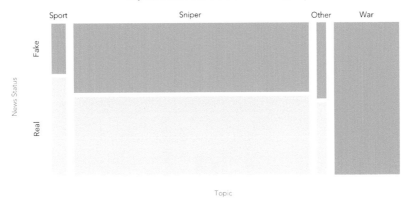

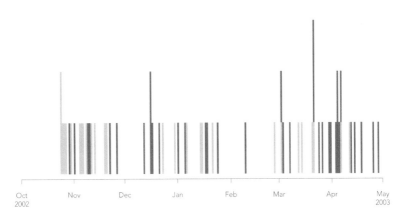

Figure 2 The Jayson Blair fake news corpus

domestic coverage of the Iraq War, he never published a real news article on that topic that meets our inclusion criteria.

Despite being uniquely well suited for the analysis of fake news, this corpus has certain limitations. First, it is small, totalling only 64 articles and 56,982 words. This directly affects the types of statistical methods we can apply. Most notably, there are too few texts to conduct a standard multidimensional register analysis. We therefore test each grammatical variable individually for differences across real and fake news, identifying sets of related variables through careful manual analysis. It is important to acknowledge, however, that our corpus is not a sample but the complete population of texts that meet our criteria. There is therefore no reason to employ inferential statistics, as we are not trying to generalise from a sample to the population: we are simply interested in describing how the act of deception affects a range of grammatical variables in Blair's writings as collected. Given our research goals, the corpus could not be any larger.

Second, there is topical variation in our corpus, including substantial variation in the rate of real and fake news across topics, as visualised in Figure 2. Given our grammatical focus, variation in topic is not a primary concern, but it may point to differences in register. For example, we might expect that Blair's reporting on the Sniper Attacks was more formal and less narrative than his reporting on the families of soldiers in Iraq. We address this concern by assessing the consistency of our results when we restrict our analysis to articles related to the Sniper Attacks; other topics are associated with too few articles or too little variation between real and fake news to allow for more holistic modelling of the effect of topic or register.

Finally, our corpus only represents the writings of one journalist. This was by design – our goal is to focus on a single author to increase confidence that observed variation is explained by deception as opposed to differences between authors or dialects – but consequently we cannot know if our results generalise to other authors. Nevertheless, we believe our approach represents an important first step in the rigorous analysis of the language of fake news, allowing us to understand with great precision patterns of stylistic variation in the writing of one author.

5 Analysis and Results

In this section, we report the results of our linguistic analysis of Jayson Blair's real and fake news. We begin by presenting our main quantitative results, testing for differences in the relative frequencies of forty-nine grammatical features between the twenty-eight real and thirty-six fake articles in our corpus. In total, we find that twenty-eight of the features show non-negligible differences across these two types, providing clear evidence of variation in Blair's style when he is telling the truth and when he is lying. We then consider each of these twenty-eight features in detail, describing how their usage differs across Blair's writings through a computer-assisted discourse analysis of the corpus. We find that variation in the use of these twenty-eight features can largely be explained by two basic differences in Blair's style: when Blair is telling the truth, he tends to write more densely and with greater conviction. We argue that these differences reflect variation in Blair's communicative intent and the production circumstances in which he wrote real and fake news.

5.1 Quantitative Results

To compare patterns of grammatical variation in Blair's real and fake news, we analysed our corpus using the Multidimensional Analysis Tagger (Nini 2019). The tagger computes normalised values for sixty-seven grammatical features across the texts in the corpus based on the feature set most commonly used in multidimensional register analysis (Biber 1988). As we are working with standard news texts, the tagger achieves over 90 per cent accuracy on our corpus. More information on the feature set and the tagger can be found in Biber (1988) and Nini (2019), including detailed descriptions of each feature. Although we use this tagset so that we can draw directly on insights from register analysis (especially Biber 1988), in practice, any sufficiently accurate part-of-speech tagger would allow for similar patterns to be broadly observed.

Out of these sixty-seven linguistic features, we excluded seventeen that occur very infrequently in our corpus (less than once per thousand words) because their low frequencies preclude the meaningful comparison of their relative frequencies across the texts in our corpus, which are mostly under 1,000 words long. We also excluded type-token ratio given the well-known issues with this measure (Baayen 2002). This left us with forty-nine normalised linguistic features for further analysis all of which are measured per hundred words, aside from average word length, which is measured as the mean number of characters per word.

To identify differences in the values of these forty-nine features measured across each of the twenty-eight real articles and the thirty-six fake articles in our corpus, we computed Cliff's delta (Cliff 1993) using the *effsize* package in R (Torchiano 2020). Cliff's delta is an ordinal measure of effect size that compares the difference in the values of a variable measured across two groups. Cliff's delta is computed by taking all pairs of values across the two groups and computing the proportion of times that the value from one group is larger than the value from the other. Specifically, Cliff's delta is calculated as

$$d = \frac{\#(x_i > x_j) - \#(x_i < x_j)}{mn}$$

where the variable x is measured across m observations for the first group and n observations for the second group, where $\#(x_i > x_j)$ is the number of times for all pairs of observations from the two groups that the value of the variable is higher for the first group, and where $\#(x_i < x_j)$ is the number of times for all pairs of observations from the two groups that the value of the variable is lower for the first group. A positive Cliff's delta simply indicates that the first group is characterised by a higher proportion of larger values than the second group, whereas a negative Cliff's delta indicates that the second group is characterised by a higher proportion of larger values than the first group.

We chose to use a non-parametric ordinal test of effect size because many of our features are positively skewed, with many texts having no occurrences of that feature. This makes more common measures of effect size like Cohen's *d* inappropriate. Cliff's delta has also been shown to be generally as powerful as Cohen's *d* when these assumptions are met (Cliff 1993), making it suitable for analysing our full feature set. We do not conduct inferential statistical analysis because our goal is only to describe variation in our corpus, which consists of the complete population of texts written by Blair that meet our criteria.

Table 2 presents the forty-nine linguistic features and the results of the main quantitative analysis conducted for this study, including median values for all texts in the corpus (with all variables aside from average word length computed as relative frequencies measured per hundred words), real texts, and fake texts, ranked by the strength of the difference between real and fake texts, as indicated by Cliff's delta. Table 2 also includes qualitative interpretations of the magnitude of the effect for each feature based on general thresholds, classifying variables as showing large ($|d| > 0.474$), medium ($|d| > 0.33$), small ($|d| > 0.147$), or negligible effects (Romano et al. 2006). Based on these criteria, we find that twenty-eight of the forty-nine features show non-negligible differences between Blair's real and fake articles, reflecting substantial linguistic differences in how Blair constructs real and fake news. Boxplots for these twenty-eight features are presented in Figures 3 to 5, sorted by effect size, with superimposed strip plots to show the full distribution of the variables across the two sets of texts. These plots show clear differences across real and fake texts.

In the remainder of this section, we examine each of these twenty-eight features in detail from a functional perspective to understand how and why Blair's writing style varies between real and fake news. For each feature we consider its communicative purpose in the English language in general, drawing on previous research in register analysis, and in Blair's writing in particular,

Table 2 Quantitative results: Main linguistic analysis

Feature	Median	Median (Real)	Median (Fake)	Q1 (Real)	Q1 (Fake)	Q3 (Real)	Q3 (Fake)	Cliff's Delta	Direction	Magnitude
Average World Length *	4.77	4.84	4.68	4.74	4.54	4.9	4.8	-0.56	Real	large
Other Nouns *	31.51	32.48	29.99	31.54	28.55	33.83	32.33	-0.49	Real	large
Nominalisations *	2.28	2.45	1.91	2.23	1.31	3.2	2.41	-0.47	Real	medium
Emphatics *	0.42	0.31	0.49	0.14	0.3	0.46	0.77	0.41	Fake	medium
Present Tense Verbs *	2.44	2.02	2.63	1.27	1.83	2.87	4.4	0.36	Fake	medium
Predicative Adjectives *	0.32	0.23	0.38	0	0.28	0.55	0.61	0.34	Fake	medium
Pronoun It *	0.39	0.33	0.48	0.11	0.23	0.42	0.7	0.33	Fake	small
Suasive Verbs *	0.42	0.58	0.28	0.27	0.21	0.9	0.54	-0.3	Real	small
WH Relatives (Subject Gap)	0.23	0.15	0.27	0.09	0.18	0.3	0.33	0.29	Fake	small
Present Participial Post-Nominals *	0.2	0.27	0.16	0.14	0.04	0.39	0.26	-0.29	Real	small
Copula Be	1.06	0.9	1.2	0.63	0.82	1.16	1.43	0.28	Fake	small
Other Subordinators *	0.14	0.08	0.14	0	0.04	0.18	0.27	0.28	Fake	small
First Person Pronouns *	0.51	0.38	0.64	0.13	0.23	0.7	1.02	0.27	Fake	small
Third Person Pronouns	3.22	2.88	3.92	2.36	2.5	3.72	5.76	0.27	Fake	small

Past Participial Post-Nominals	0.19	0.26	0.16	0.14	0	0.34	0.29	−0.26	Real	small
Gerunds	0.84	1.1	0.7	0.64	0.42	1.46	1.01	−0.25	Real	small
Perfect Aspect	1.05	0.95	1.08	0.55	0.69	1.25	1.65	0.25	Fake	small
Place Adverbials	0.3	0.25	0.35	0.14	0.24	0.52	0.49	0.24	Fake	small
Second Person Pronouns *	0.06	0	0.1	0	0	0.17	0.32	0.23	Fake	small
By Passives	0.14	0.16	0.12	0.1	0	0.24	0.18	−0.22	Real	small
Prediction Modals *	0.42	0.48	0.38	0.26	0.23	0.8	0.57	−0.22	Real	small
Demonstrative Pronouns	0.25	0.22	0.28	0	0.17	0.32	0.38	0.19	Fake	small
Public Verbs	2.32	2.51	2.17	1.98	1.92	2.87	2.62	−0.19	Real	small
Split Auxiliaries *	0.23	0.22	0.24	0	0.15	0.39	0.43	0.19	Fake	small
Infinitive To	1.73	1.73	1.73	1.51	1.15	2.25	2.11	−0.19	Real	small
Downtoners	0.14	0.1	0.16	0	0.04	0.22	0.26	0.18	Fake	small
Time Adverbials	0.56	0.6	0.51	0.52	0.4	0.87	0.93	−0.18	Real	small
Attributive Adjectives	3.86	3.52	4.03	3.19	3.38	4.63	4.79	0.16	Fake	small
Causative Subordinators	0.11	0.14	0.09	0	0	0.25	0.17	−0.14	Real	negligible
Possibility Modals	0.32	0.3	0.36	0.17	0.18	0.47	0.58	0.14	Fake	negligible

Table 2 (cont.)

Feature	Median	Median (Real)	Median (Fake)	Q1 (Real)	Q1 (Fake)	Q3 (Real)	Q3 (Fake)	Cliff's Delta	Direction	Magnitude
Adverbs	2.08	1.94	2.19	1.55	1.67	2.34	2.63	0.14	Fake	negligible
Verb Complement That	0.7	0.74	0.66	0.5	0.44	1.1	0.9	−0.14	Real	negligible
Private Verbs	1.19	1.09	1.27	0.79	0.83	1.52	1.54	0.13	Fake	negligible
That Relatives (Subject Gap)	0.22	0.26	0.16	0.17	0.11	0.34	0.33	−0.13	Real	negligible
Clausal Coordination	0.35	0.34	0.41	0.21	0.17	0.42	0.55	0.12	Fake	negligible
That Relatives (Object Gap)	0.3	0.33	0.27	0.24	0.13	0.4	0.46	−0.1	Real	negligible
Phrasal Coordination	0.68	0.66	0.69	0.45	0.51	0.87	0.88	0.09	Fake	negligible
Sentence Relatives *	0.08	0.08	0.09	0	0	0.16	0.18	0.09	Fake	negligible
Existential There	0.14	0.14	0.14	0	0.04	0.23	0.21	0.08	Fake	negligible
Agentless Passives *	1.54	1.54	1.61	1.2	1.26	2.04	1.99	0.08	Fake	negligible
Complement That Deletion *	0.54	0.56	0.52	0.3	0.34	0.94	0.83	−0.08	Real	negligible
Analytic Negation	0.64	0.58	0.68	0.44	0.4	0.92	0.95	0.08	Fake	negligible
Demonstrative Determiners	0.74	0.74	0.72	0.55	0.5	1.09	0.91	−0.07	Real	negligible
Prepositions	10.64	10.59	10.79	9.92	10.06	11.15	11.41	0.06	Fake	negligible

WH Complements	0.07	0	0.08	0	0	0.16	0.18	0.06	Fake	negligible
Conditional Subordinators *	0.14	0.12	0.14	0	0	0.24	0.2	0.05	Fake	negligible
Contractions	0.19	0.16	0.2	0.08	0	0.32	0.4	0.05	Fake	negligible
Present Participial	0.13	0.13	0.12	0	0	0.2	0.28	0.02	Fake	negligible
Past Tense Verbs	6.59	6.58	6.59	5.45	5.52	7.56	7.98	0.01	Fake	negligible

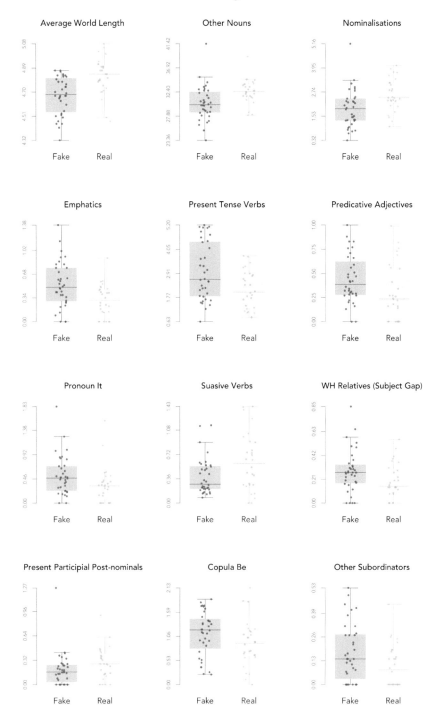

Figure 3 Feature boxplots (Part 1)

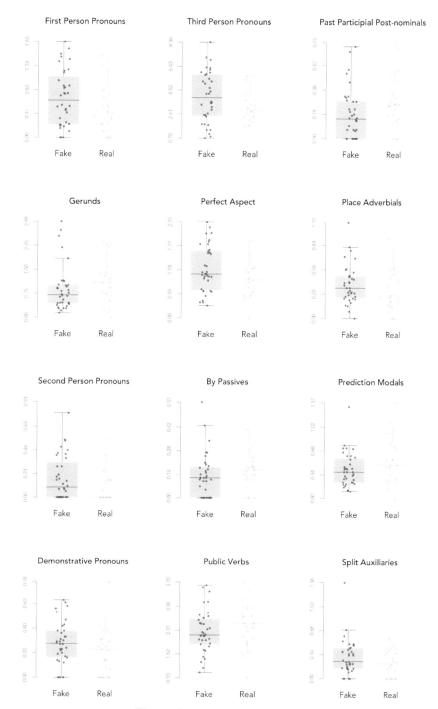

Figure 4 Feature boxplots (Part 2)

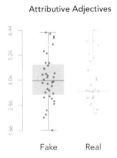

Figure 5 Feature boxplots (Part 3)

through a close analysis of its use in the corpus, supported with numerous examples. Our goal is to identify sets of features that show systematic differences, reflecting variation in Blair's specific communicative goals and the effect of the specific communicative contexts in which he wrote real and fake news. In this way, we can provide evidence that what we observe is not just random variation, but systematic patterns in grammatical variation, as commonly identified in register analysis.

In addition, Table 2 highlights the features that show non-negligible differences when we restrict our comparison to the twenty-five real and twenty fake articles on the D.C. Sniper Attacks (marked with an asterisk). We present this additional information so as to help us assess whether the general patterns we identify remain stable when we further control for variation in topic/register. We find that fourteen of these twenty-eight features show non-negligible differences in the Sniper articles, including nine of the top ten features. We also find four additional features that show substantial differences in only the D.C. Sniper texts. Notably, in all cases, all features trend in the same direction, even if the magnitude of the difference changes. Overall, the results are therefore largely consistent, especially considering the decrease in the number of observations.

We discuss these differences in greater detail as we consider the overall patterns of stylistic variation we have identified.

5.2 Information Density

Of the twenty-eight features that show non-negligible differences between Blair's real and fake news, twenty-three are associated with variation in information density. Blair's real news contains more frequent use of a range of features that are characteristic of denser texts, like academic writing and newspaper reporting, where authors express large amounts of detailed information in a limited space and have time to edit their texts to achieve high levels of concision (Chafe 1982, 1985; Biber 1988). Most commonly, this involves creating long and complex noun phrases to maximise the amount of information that can be packed into sentences. Alternatively, Blair's fake news contains fewer nouns and noun modifiers, but more features associated with an interactive and spontaneous style of discourse, including pronouns, verbs, and adverbs. This is not to say that the structure of Blair's real and fake news differs markedly. All Blair's articles are written in a relatively dense style as is standard for newspaper articles, making them difficult to distinguish. We find, however, that Blair tends to shift towards a slightly less dense style in his fake news. We discuss this pattern in this section, considering each of these twenty-three features individually.

5.2.1 Real News Features

The most distinctive feature between Blair's real and fake news is ***Average Word Length***, which tends to be substantially longer in his real news. Word length is clearly linked to information density: in general, longer words are more frequent in registers that prioritise efficient communication because longer words, especially nouns, tend to convey more complex information; alternatively, shorter words, including many common words, are more frequent in registers that are spontaneous and interactive like conversations (Biber 1988). For instance, consider the following four examples, which are relatively long sentences (over twenty words) with especially low and high average word lengths:

1. *He says he is committed to giving her all of his time when the war is over and he gets to go home.* (F33)

2. *"If this evidence is going to be used to tie into the fact that our client was there that night, I think we can show that he was not," Mr. Petit said.* (R18)

3. *The judge, LeRoy F. Millette Jr. of Prince William County Circuit Court, denied a request by the Radio-Television News Directors Association and*

> *several broadcast stations, which was opposed by prosecutors and lawyers for Mr. Muhammad.* (F07)

4. *The detention hearings bring the Justice Department one step closer to making a determination about which jurisdiction where sniper attacks occurred will proceed first.* (R07)

Examples 1 and 2, which have very low average word lengths (3.3 and 3.4 characters per word), are representations of spoken language. Alternatively, examples 3 and 4, which have very high average word lengths (5.4 and 5.8 characters per word), are much denser. This difference can be better appreciated by comparing the proportion of content words to function words in these examples: content words account for seven out of twenty-three words (30 per cent) and eight out of twenty-nine words (28 per cent) in the first two sentences, whereas they account for twenty-five out of thirty-six words (69 per cent) and fourteen out of twenty-four words (58 per cent) in the second two sentences. Consequently, the second two sentences effectively express more information per word.

The second most distinctive feature we have identified is the relative frequency of **Nouns**, which tend to be substantially more common in Blair's real news. Nouns are a central feature of texts with high levels of information density for two primary reasons. First, we use nouns to convey specific information about people, places, and things. Second, we tend to incorporate additional information into sentences by modifying nouns, often using nouns as pre-modifiers or using phrases and clauses that contain nouns as post-modifiers. For instance, consider examples 1 and 2, which have much shorter average word lengths, and which are characterised by far fewer nouns, in each case accounting for around 15 per cent of the words in these sentences, compared to examples 3 and 4, which have much longer average word lengths, and which are characterised by 61 per cent and 38 per cent nouns. Overall, sentences that contain a higher proportion of nouns are more common in Blair's real news, indicative of a more informationally dense style of writing.

In addition to nouns in general, Blair's real articles also tend to contain more frequent use of various noun types, which are excluded from our general noun count. Most notably, **Nominalisations**, which are the third most distinctive feature we have analysed, tend to be substantially more common in Blair's real news. Nominalisations are a type of noun that contain certain derivational suffixes, most commonly *-tion*, *-ment*, *-ness*, and *-ity*, all of which can be used to convert a verb into a noun (although many of these nouns were directly borrowed into English, e.g. from French). Like other nouns, nominalisations are associated with a denser style of writing, especially as they often provide an economical way to refer to complex ideas. For instance, example 4 contains four words tagged as nominalisations (*detention, department, determination, jurisdiction*), where each of these words refer to very abstract concepts.

Similarly, **Gerunds**, which are *-ing* forms of verbs used as nouns, also tend to occur more frequently in Blair's real news. Like nominalisations, gerunds allow for information to be communicated more efficiently by placing greater informational burden on nouns than verbs, expressing concepts that are underlyingly related to actions as nouns. For instance, the word *hearings* in example 4 is a gerund, referencing an entire event using a single noun. This gerund is also pre-modified by the nominalisation *detention,* illustrating how nouns are not only modified to increase density in a text, but act as pre-nominal modifiers themselves – a hallmark of a highly informational style.

Several features associated with post-nominal modification are also more frequent in Blair's real news. Post-nominal modification involves the use of phrases and clauses following a noun to incorporate additional information into the noun phrase. This is often how long noun phrases are constructed in English. Three types of post-nominal modification show substantial differences between Blair's real and fake news, but almost all relevant features trend in this direction. The most distinctive are **Present Participial Post-Nominals** and **Past Participial Post-Nominals**, each of which consists of a verb phrase, headed by a verb in either its present (*-ing*) or past (*-ed/-en*) participial form, most often followed by a noun phrase object, where the noun being post-modified acts like the subject of the verb. For instance, consider examples 5 and 6:

5. *The task force examining the sniper attacks that left 10 dead in the Washington area has uncovered fingerprints placing one defendant, John Muhammad, at the scene of one shooting, but still have little evidence suggesting that he pulled the trigger in any of the killings, law enforcement officials said today.* (F13)

6. *Defense lawyers filed an exhibit list that included orders filed at courts in Baltimore and Fairfax appointing defense lawyers and guardians.* (R28)

In example 5, there are three different present participial post-nominals, which are headed by the verbs *examining* (modifying *force*), *placing* (modifying *fingerprints*), and *suggesting* (modifying *evidence*). Alternatively, example 6 contains both a past and a present participial post-nominal (headed by *filed* and *appointing*), both of which modify the same noun (*orders*).

These examples illustrate how this type of post-nominal modification creates very long, dense, and complex sentences. Notably, both examples also contain instances of *That Relatives* (*that left ten dead . . ., that included order . . .*), a closely related form of post-nominal modification, illustrating how such structures tend to co-occur together in texts and sentences. Although these features do not show substantial differences between real and fake news, they trend in the same direction. It is also notable that the closely related feature *WH Relatives* does not show this same pattern, occurring substantially more often in fake news. We return to this surprising result in Section 5.3.

Similarly, the use of **Infinitive To**, which heads infinitive phrases consisting of *to* followed by a verb phrase, tends to be substantially more common in Blair's real news. Infinitive phrases are generally associated with idea expansion (Biber 1988), including through post-nominal modification, although they can have a wide range of other functions. For instance, in example 1, the infinitive phrase *to go home* is acting as an argument of the verb *gets*. Example 7, however, illustrates how an infinitive phrase (*to extort money*) can be used to modify a noun (*plot*):

7. *Federal prosecutors in Maryland brought charges against Mr. Muhammad, 41, and Mr. Malvo last week, saying the shootings were part of a plot to extort money.* (R08)

We find that Blair's use of infinitives shows the largest difference between real and fake news when Blair uses infinitive phrases to modify nouns – or at least when they occur following a noun, as opposed to an adjective, a verb, or another word class. Specifically, infinitive *to* following a noun occurs at a rate of 0.55 per hundred words in Blair's real news, compared to 0.40 per hundred words in his fake news, whereas he uses infinitive *to* at an equal if not higher rate in his fake news following other word classes.

Finally, although most adverbial forms are more common in Blair's fake news, as we discuss below, **Time Adverbials** (e.g. *afterwards, again, now*) tend to be substantially more common in Blair's real news. For instance, consider examples 8 and 9, which each contain two time adverbials (*now, today, yesterday*):

8. *The police stopped the men who are now charged in the sniper shootings at least three times, including once here for suspicious behavior, during the three-week rampage, law enforcement officials said today.* (R03)

9. *But one of the defense team members said yesterday that they now had evidence that detectives "knew that they should not have been questioning him."* (R21)

As these examples illustrate, in general, Blair often used time adverbials to concisely add information about when the events being reported took place, which is basic information in any newspaper article. Time adverbials can therefore also be associated with informationally dense news texts.

Overall, we therefore find Blair's real articles are characterised by more frequent use of various grammatical features associated with informationally dense discourse, especially features that are related to nouns and noun modification. This is precisely the style we would expect in newspaper writing, and both Blair's real and fake articles are characterised by a relatively dense style, as is presumably the case for almost all articles published by *The New York Times*. Blair's overall use of these features, however, is higher in his real articles – a subtle but robust difference in his style when he writes real and fake news. Alternatively, Blair's fake articles are not only characterised by less frequent use of these nominal features, but by more frequent use of many features associated with a more informal and spontaneous style of discourse, including a range of pronouns, verbs, adverbs, and subordinators.

5.2.2 Fake News Features

In terms of fake news features, we find most notably that Blair uses five different types of pronouns at substantially higher rates in his fake news. Given the frequent use of nouns in his real news, this result is not a surprise. In general, a noun phrase can be headed by a noun or a pronoun, and therefore frequent use of nouns tends to imply infrequent use of pronouns and vice versa. Pronouns are also much less amenable to modification. Alternatively, pronouns allow for links to be made across texts by efficiently referencing entities previously mentioned in the discourse, which is especially important for spontaneous language production. Texts with relatively high pronoun frequency are therefore generally associated with a less informationally dense style (Biber 1988). For example, frequent pronoun use is characteristic of conversations and more informal written registers, at least in part because these contexts tend to provide less time for planning and editing. This makes it more difficult to construct complex noun phrases, resulting in information that might otherwise be contained in one sentence being spread across several sentences that are linked together by pronouns, which do not add any new information into the discourse.

Pronoun It is the most distinctive pronoun feature under analysis and the seventh most distinctive feature we have identified, occurring substantially more often in Blair's fake news. For instance, examples 10 and 11 contain numerous tokens of pronoun *it*:

10. *It broke, and he fixed it by pulling out the fuse and wiring it with a paper clip.* (F33)

11. *"You never know. It happens all the time where we pass a law and then prosecutors will abuse it. And it forces us to decide whether to come back at it and rein it in a bit."* (F09)

In these examples, we can see how *it* is used to connect entities within and across sentences. In example 10, which is presented as reported speech, *it* refers three times to a computer being fixed by a soldier. Consider how this sentence, which contains two conjoined independent clauses, could be recast as a single noun phrase (e.g. *the broken computer fixed by replacing the fuse with a paperclip*). This noun phrase could then be inserted into a sentence, substantially increasing the information density of this text. Similarly, in example 11, which is presented as quoted speech, *it* is used five times across two sentences. The first token acts as a dummy pronoun, referring to nothing: the first six words of the example could be replaced by the word *often* with no real loss of information. Alternatively, the third token essentially links back to the entire first sentence, while the other three reference *law*.

The other **Third Person Pronouns**, which are generally used for human referents (*she, he, they, her, him, them, his, their, himself, herself, themselves*), follow this same pattern. These words are very common across the entire corpus: no matter how densely it is written, almost any newspaper article will need to repeatedly refer to specific people across sentences and paragraphs, and this generally can be achieved most concisely using third person pronouns. These words, however, are especially frequent in Blair's fake news, reflecting lower overall use of complex noun phrases. For instance, consider example 12, a single sentence that contains five tokens of *he*, as well as two tokens of *his*, which act like a determiner:

12. *Explaining that he felt that his sense of safety and security "was taken away in an instant" on the day of the attack, the corporal said he told the chaplain in an hour-and-a-half conversation that he worried that long after he recovered physically he would struggle with the images in his head.* (F34)

Crucially, each token of *he* acts as a simple noun phrase with no modification, substantially lowering the potential information density of this sentence. Notably, third person pronouns are often associated with narratives (Biber 1988). However, although Blair, like many reporters, often employs a narrative style, as in this example, variation in narration does not appear to explain the differences in third person pronoun usage we observe, given that the relative frequency of past tense verbs, the most basic characteristic of narratives, is the least distinctive of all the features we have considered.

Similarly, ***Demonstrative Pronouns*** (*this, that, these, those*) are also substantially more common in Blair's fake news. For instance, example 13 contains two tokens of *this* used as a demonstrative pronoun:

13. *"But people are often surprised by how it takes a hold of them. Everyone is human. It can't help but take an effect on people when they're seeing things like this and seeing it in numbers like this."* (F26)

In this quoted passage, both uses of *this* are referring to the Iraq War, although their exact references are not absolutely clear, even after reading the entire article, and even if we assume this quote is real. The three uses of *it*, all of which also refer to the Iraq War, are also notable. The way these pronouns work together to create a series of sentences that are intricately linked to each other is highly complex, but this information could be expressed more concisely, rather than being spread out across several sentences.

Finally, Blair's use of ***First Person Pronouns*** (*I, me, us, my, we, our, myself, ourselves*) and ***Second Person Pronouns*** (*you, your, yourself, yourselves*) are especially distinctive, with both types of pronouns being substantially more common in Blair's fake news. Notably, Blair uses both types of pronouns almost exclusively inside quotations. Specifically, 98 per cent of first person pronouns occur within quotations in his real news and over 99 per cent in his fake news, and all second person pronouns occur within quotations in his real and fake news. Alternatively, only 11 per cent and 13 per cent of third person pronouns occur within quotations in his real and fake news. In other words, not only do his fake news articles contain more pronouns in general, but they also contain more first and second person pronouns *in quotations*. This result implies that when Blair fabricates quotes, he also writes them in a less dense style than what is found in his real news. Relatedly, the overall percentage of words in Blair's real and fake articles that occur inside quotations is relatively small and similar, at 12 per cent in real articles and 15 per cent in fake articles, implying that general stylistic differences between quoted and unquoted texts do not primarily explain our results.

In addition to pronouns, Blair's fake news is also characterised by more frequent use of a variety of verbs. The co-occurrence of pronominal and verbal forms is to be expected: as a text uses less complex noun phrases and relies more on pronouns, main verbs also become more common, as independent clauses, which must have a main verb at their core, become shorter. For instance, consider example 12, which contains four tokens of the pronoun *he,* each of which is followed immediately by a verb. Most notably, ***Present Tense***, which is the fifth most distinctive feature we have identified, is considerably more common in Blair's fake news and is generally associated with a more informal and interactive style (Biber 1988).

The use of **Perfect Aspect** and **Copula Be** follow this same pattern. *Copula Be* is especially interesting as it is used to provide additional information about the noun phrase subject, much like noun modification; however, it does this outside the noun phrase, reducing the overall density of a text. For instance, consider example 14:

14. *At court hearings for Mr. Malvo, who is charged in Ms. Franklin's death, Mr. Franklin has sat silently behind prosecutors. He was the only relative of a victim to testify at a hearing to determine whether Mr. Malvo should be tried as an adult.* (F17)

These two sentences could be combined by directly incorporating the information about Mr. Franklin in the second sentence into the noun phrase in the first sentence where he is initially referenced (e.g. *Mr. Franklin, who was the only relative . . .*).

This pattern also helps explain the more frequent use of **Predicative Adjectives** in Blair's fake news, as these adjectives must follow a copula. However, **Attributive Adjectives**, which pre-modify a noun, are also more common in Blair's fake news, seemingly contradicting the overall tendency for noun modifiers to occur more often in Blair's real news. Although attributive adjectives do allow for additional information to be incorporated into noun phrases, they are often avoided in news writing. This is because they tend to add inconsequential information while risking weakening or editorialising statements. *The New York Times* (Yagoda 2007) even published an excerpt on avoiding adjectives from Yagoda (2006), a book titled *When You Catch an Adjective Kill It: Parts of Speech, for Better And/Or Worse*. For this reason, the frequent use of adjectives in general can be seen as effectively lowering the information density of newspaper writing.

Blair's fake news also shows more frequent use of many types of adverbs, which are often considered unnecessary for similar reasons. Most notably, Blair uses **Emphatics** (e.g. *very, extremely*), the fourth most distinctive feature we have identified, at a considerably higher rate in fake news. Emphatics are used to mark emphasis, especially on adjectives, and are therefore generally associated with more informal and interactive contexts (Biber 1988). Similarly, Blair also uses **Downtoners** (e.g. *nearly, slightly*) and so-called **Place Adverbials**, which include adverbs and prepositions (e.g. ab*ove, nearby, outside*), at substantially higher rates in his fake news. In addition, **Split Auxiliaries**, which are created by inserting an adverb between an auxiliary verb and a main verb, occur more often in Blair's fake news, reflecting the higher use of both verbs and adverbs in these texts. The (other) *Adverb* feature we considered also trends in this direction, but does not show as clear of a pattern.

Finally, (other) **Subordinators** are substantially more common in Blair's fake news, which include words like *since, while* and *whereas*. Subordinators head subordinate clauses, which contain an independent clause. In this way, they allow for independent clauses to be joined together, as illustrated in example 15, where the subordinator *while* heads the initial subordinate clause:

15. *While some of those enlisted in this work ask not to return, most come back for additional tours, Lieutenant Milhoan said.* (F26)

Once again, building meaning through combining entire clauses, rather than incorporating information into phrases, is characteristic of less informationally dense texts, especially registers of spoken language (Biber et al. 2020). The increased use of subordinators in Blair's fake news is therefore consistent with our overall interpretation of grammatical variation in Blair's writing. Other more specific categories of subordinators do not show clear patterns, although *Conditional Subordinators* (i.e. *if* and *unless*) trend in this direction, and show a non-negligible difference between Blair's real and fake news when we restrict our analysis to the articles on the sniper attacks.

5.2.3 Summary

Overall, twenty-three of the twenty-eight grammatical features that show non-negligible differences between Blair's real and fake news are therefore related to information density. Specifically, eight features (Average Word Length, Nouns, Nominalisations, Gerunds, Present Participial Post-Nominals, Past Participial Post-Nominals, Infinitive To, Time Adverbials) are more common in his real news, and fifteen features (Pronoun It, Demonstrative Pronouns, Third Person Pronouns, First Person Pronouns, Second Person Pronouns, Present Tense, Perfect Aspect, Copula Be, Predicative Adjectives, Attributive Adjectives, Emphatics, Downtoners, Place Adverbials, Split Auxiliaries, Subordinators) are more common in his fake news. Furthermore, twelve of these features continue to show non-negligible differences when we restrict our analysis to the articles on the sniper attacks, providing further evidence that these results represent robust differences between Blair's real and fake news, which are not confounded by variation in topic or other forms of register variation. We therefore observe subtle variation in Blair's style of reporting, which we interpret as being related to variation in the level of information density in Blair's real and fake news.

Crucially, we believe this pattern can be explained by variation in Blair's communicative intent and the communicative context in which he wrote these texts. A dense style is the standard for newspaper writing because it allows for detailed information to be conveyed in a limited space (Biber 1988). Writing in this style, however, is challenging because the author must construct complex noun phrases, which tend to require planning and editing. Given these factors, it appears that Blair's style may have become less dense in his fake news for two reasons. First, based on his own statements, it appears Blair was under pressure to write articles quickly, and it therefore seems likely that he had less opportunity to carefully plan and edit his fake news to maximise their density. Second, Blair had less real information to convey in his fake news and therefore may not have been as concerned about writing densely. In fact, it was presumably to his advantage to write less dense texts, as it would place less pressure on him to construct more detailed deceptions. Blair appears to have adopted a somewhat less informationally dense style when writing fake news as a solution to his communicative problem – to quickly produce news articles that were not based directly on real reporting.

5.3 Conviction

Although twenty-three of the twenty-eight linguistic features we have considered that show non-negligible differences between Blair's real and fake news can be linked to his use of a denser style of communication when he is telling the truth, five features do not conform to this pattern. In fact, these features trend in the opposite direction: *WH Relatives* are more common in his fake news but involve noun modification, whereas *Suasive Verbs, Possibility Modals, By-Passives,* and *Public Verbs* are more common in his real news but involve verbs. These features are therefore highly marked, going against Blair's general tendency to use more nominal forms in real news and more verbal forms in fake news. All five of these features, however, can be associated with *stance* – how a speaker or an author expresses their assessments, attitudes, and opinions towards the information they are communicating (Biber & Finegan 1989; Gray & Biber 2012). A number of these features can also be associated more specifically with *evidentiality,* which is how languages mark information about the source of an utterance and the reliability of the knowledge being conveyed (Aikhenvald 2004). In some languages this is achieved through obligatory grammatical marking, for example, encoding information about whether or not an event was witnessed directly by the speaker. In English, however, this information is optional, communicated obliquely through a wide range of grammatical, lexical, and discursive strategies (Chafe 1986; Biber & Finegan 1989). We find that Blair's real and fake news differs in terms of how these strategies are deployed. In particular, in our opinion, Blair writes real news with greater *conviction* than fake news, adopting a more persuasive and confident stance towards both the information he is reporting and his sources. In this section, we consider Blair's use of these five features, as well as *Agentless Passive*, a feature that shows substantial differences when we restrict our analysis to the articles on the Sniper Attacks. We also revisit Blair's use of the

Perfect Aspect and *Downtoners*, as they are directly linked to the expression of evidentiality as well as information density.

5.3.1 Real News Features

The most distinctive feature that we have not yet discussed is **Suasive Verbs** (e.g. *allow, decide, determine, propose*), which are substantially more frequent in Blair's real news. Suasive verbs are often used to describe an action that is intended to actuate some kind of change and are therefore often associated with persuasive texts (Biber 1988). As a reporter, however, Blair is not generally using these words to persuade the reader of the validity of his personal views; rather, he is conveying his assessment of the likelihood of the events he is covering resulting in change. For instance, consider examples 16 and 17:

16. *Law enforcement officials said Attorney General John Ashcroft would most likely decide this week which jurisdiction should proceed with the first case against the two.* (R08)

17. *During the first day of a hearing that will determine whether Mr. Malvo, 17, faces charges that could bring a death sentence, he heard of the pain caused by the killing with which he is charged.* (R18)

In both sentences, Blair uses a suasive verb (*decide, determine*) to describe a future action that will have legal consequences and to express his assessment of how likely that event is to take place. Notably, in example 16, Blair specifies that this information is coming from law enforcement officials. Through his frequent use of *Suasive Verbs* in real news, Blair is therefore conveying a level of confidence in the information he is reporting and in his sources: he is writing with conviction.

Similarly, **Prediction Modals** (*will, would*), which are associated with the expression of stance (Biber & Finegan 1989; Gray & Biber 2012), also tend to occur more frequently in Blair's real news. Even more directly than *suasive verbs*, these forms are used to refer to possible future events and outcomes with high levels of certainty. For instance, Blair uses these modals in examples 16 and 17 preceding the two suasive verbs previously highlighted, expressing a high level of confidence in the likely outcomes of the event he is covering. This type of language is especially notable in newspaper reporting, as the goal is generally to focus on describing newsworthy events that have recently taken place *in the past*; discussing the likely outcomes of these events in the future can therefore be seen as a more marked communicative choice that directly imbues an article with a higher level of conviction.

Blair's use of the passive voice is also related to the expression of conviction. Passives are used to emphasise the entity being acted upon by the verb, making it the grammatical subject of the sentence, as opposed to the agent engaging in the action. Blair uses **By Passives**, which include the agent in a *by*-phrase, substantially more often in his real news. This construction is illustrated in example 18.

18. *Mr. Malvo's court-appointed guardian, Todd G. Petit, tried to halt the questioning, but was rebuffed by both the police and prosecutors.* (R28)

In this sentence, the passive voice is used to highlight that Malvo's guardian was *rebuffed*, but a *by*-phrase is also included that identifies transparently who was doing the rebuffing (*the police and prosecutors*). No information is therefore lost compared to the corresponding sentence in the active voice (e.g. *The police and prosecutors rebuffed Petit*). The use of *By Passives* can therefore be associated with the transparent identification of the people involved in the news being reported and the sources of this information.

Alternatively, Blair uses **Agentless Passives,** which omit the agent, and are often used to obscure the agent in newspaper writing for various reasons (Blanco-Gómez 2002), more often in his fake news – substantially more often if we restrict our analysis to the articles on the sniper attacks. This construction is illustrated in example 19.

19. *In Mr. Malvo's case, other law enforcement officials said today that even if Mr. Malvo's admissions were thrown out by a judge who determined that he had been denied his rights to counsel and a guardian at the time he was questioned, there is enough evidence, including computer files on a laptop that was recovered when the men were arrested, to convict him of killing Ms. Franklin.* (F04)

In this sentence, four passives are used in one sentence (*were thrown out, had been denied, was questioned, was recovered*), including only one *by*-passive (*by the judge*). The other three examples are agentless passives, and it is not entirely clear who did the *denying, questioning,* or *recovering,* substantially increasing the imprecision of this sentence. The use of *Agentless Passives,* as opposed to *By Passives,* therefore increases the amount of uncertainty in the text.

Public Verbs are also substantially more common in Blair's real news and can be directly related to the expression of conviction. This semantic class of verbs involves actions that are observed publicly, specifically speech acts (e.g. *agree, report, suggest*). By far the most common public verbs used across Blair's news are forms of the verb *to say,* which accounts for 76 per cent of the 1,296 tokens of public verbs across our full corpus. Public verbs are regularly used by Blair to introduce direct and indirect quotations, as illustrated in examples 20 and 21.

20. *"In essence," Mr. Horan said, "they were saying: 'Do you want us to stop killing people? Then give us the money.'"* (R19)

21. *Sgt. Joseph C. Gentile, a spokesman for the Washington police, said witnesses reported seeing a burgundy Toyota leaving the scene of that shooting.* (R03)

In both examples, there are two public verbs, including three tokens of *say* and one token of *report,* with three tokens in the past tense. The first example is presented as quoted speech, including a quotation within a quotation, while the second example is presented as reported speech. The use of public verbs is one way journalists attribute the information they report to specific people, effectively marking information as second-hand knowledge. If a specific source is named, this information can then be checked for accuracy, as was done for *The New York Times* investigation. For all these reasons, using public verbs, especially when stating the source, can be interpreted as a sign of conviction – being transparent about the status of the information being reported.

The pattern, however, is much more complex. Although public verbs are more common overall in Blair's real news, Blair uses more quotations in his fake news, both in terms of the rate of quotation and the overall amount of text in quotation. These results seem incommensurate. We therefore compared Blair's use of individual public verbs in his real and fake news, as well as public verbs grouped by tense and aspect. We repeated the Cliff's delta analysis for these features (relative frequencies per hundred words) and found two opposing trends hidden by the overall public verb counts. Table 3 presents the results for the eleven features that show non-negligible differences between Blair's real and fake news, as well as the two quotation metrics, ranked by strength of the difference. Note that means for real and fake news are reported as opposed to medians, as presented in Table 3, because a number of these features are very infrequent, resulting in medians of 0 for real and fake news. Box plots for a selection of these features are also presented in Figure 6, where medians are marked.

On the one hand, the two most distinctive features are the use of public verbs in the present tense and the use of *says* more specifically, but surprisingly these forms are *more common* in Blair's fake news, going against the general trend for public verbs. Remarkably, Blair uses *says* fifty-six times in his fake news, generally to introduce quotations or reported speech, but only *once* in his real news, where it is used to quote a report as opposed to a person. In a sense, the use of *says* is therefore the most distinctive pattern we have identified. This use of *says* is illustrated in examples 22 and 23, for both quoted and reported speech.

Table 3 Quantitative results: Public verb analysis

Feature	Mean	Mean (Real)	Mean (Fake)	Q1 (Real)	Q1 (Fake)	Q3 (Real)	Q3 (Fake)	Cliff's Delta	Direction	Magnitude
Third Person Present Tense Public Verbs	0.08	0.01	0.13	0	0	0	0.15	0.36	Fake	medium
Says	0.06	0.01	0.1	0	0	0	0.1	0.27	Fake	small
Quotations Mark Relative Frequency	0.94	0.85	1	0.51	0.76	1.18	1.22	0.24	Fake	small
Progressive Voice Public Verbs	0.12	0.15	0.09	0	0	0.2	0.13	−0.22	Real	small
Agree (All forms)	0.02	0.04	0	0	0	0	0	−0.21	Real	small
Agreed	0.02	0.04	0	0	0	0	0	−0.21	Real	small
Past Tense Public Verbs	1.88	2	1.78	1.57	1.39	2.29	2.28	−0.19	Real	small
All Public Verbs	2.35	2.45	2.27	1.98	1.91	2.87	2.63	−0.19	Real	small
Suggest (All forms)	0.03	0.01	0.05	0	0	0	0.08	0.18	Fake	small
Said	1.47	1.56	1.4	1.25	1.01	1.98	1.9	−0.17	Real	small
Say (All forms)	1.76	1.81	1.72	1.56	1.39	2.19	2.07	−0.15	Real	small
Percentage of Text in Quotations	13.33	12.5	13.97	6.95	8.52	16.53	18.63	0.15	Fake	small
Saying	0.04	0.05	0.03	0	0	0.12	0.01	−0.15	Real	small

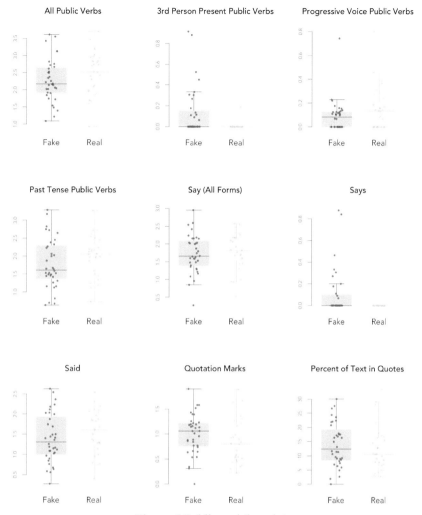

Figure 6 Public verb boxplots

22. *"I am not sure what's worse, the fear or the loneliness," Ms. Thompson says of the recent nights without her husband, Cpl. Alan Thompson, a member of a Marine artillery battalion that was among the first to enter Iraq.* (F33)

23. *At moments, Ms. Anguiano says, she can picture her son in an Iraqi village, like the ones she has seen on television, surrounded by animals and the Iraqi people he has befriended.* (F35)

The only other non-negligible feature that is more common in Blair's fake news is use of the verb *to suggest*, which seems to be broadly in line with lower levels of conviction in his fake news. On the other hand, the other eight of these features are more common in his real news, driving the overall pattern for public verbs. Most notably, these features include *said,* which is used in the simple past tense in the vast majority of cases, as illustrated in examples 20 and 21, and which is by far the most frequent of all the individual forms of public verbs.

The main pattern for public verbs is therefore Blair's more frequent use of past tense forms, especially *said,* in his real news, and Blair's more frequent use of present tense forms, especially *says,* in his fake news. In general, Blair is using these public verbs to report information he has obtained from his sources, although we know that he has often fabricated this information in his fake news. Blair therefore appears to be unwittingly encoding evidentiality into his real and fake news through his inflection of the verb *to say*: he uses the present tense almost exclusively in articles where he is lying. This pattern is not without motivation. Past tense appears to be the standard in newspaper writing for quotations from human sources; it certainly is his standard when writing real news. Blair's use of present tense *says* is therefore inherently marked. More generally, it appears that using the present tense to introduce reported information can be used in English to express doubt. Consider, for example, the sentences *he said he will come* and *he says he will come*, where the use of the present tense in the second example can imply that there is some doubt about the validity of the statement. The fact that Blair uses the present tense to introduce quotations only in his fake news therefore appears to inadvertently signal that he has less confidence in the validity of the quotes, subtly reflecting a lower level of conviction.

Overall, we can therefore see how Blair's use of a range of different grammatical features marks stance in his real news. The use of both suasive verbs and prediction modals reflects Blair's confidence that what he is covering is not only accurate but consequential, while his use of by-passives and public verbs allows Blair to explicitly identify and attribute information to his sources, which is often crucial information for establishing the validity of reporting. We believe that both these patterns, which are deployed substantially less often by Blair in his fake news, result in his real news conveying higher levels of conviction.

5.3.2 Fake News Features

While Blair's real news is characterised by frequent use of a number of features associated with greater conviction, his fake news contains not only fewer of these features, but more frequent use of features that can be associated with a less confident stance. In addition to his use of *Agentless Passives*, Blair also tends to use the ***Perfect Aspect*** (i.e. a form of the verb *have* as an auxiliary) more frequently in his fake articles. This pattern can be explained at least in part by an increased proportion of verbs in his fake news, as discussed in the previous section in relation to information density, but *Perfect Aspect* is also generally associated with the indirect expression of evidentiality cross-linguistically (Izvorski 1997), as well as in English more specifically, as illustrated in example 24.

24. *To attract Hispanic residents, the university has held fiesta-themed parties that some critics have said bordered on patronizing.* (F05)

In this case, the perfect aspect (*the university has held . . ., some critics have said . . .*) is being used to encode a level of uncertainty. If the perfect auxiliaries were removed, the sentence would read as if the parties were unequivocally no longer being held and no longer bordering on patronising. The use of the perfect aspect in this example therefore has the effect of implying that these parties *might* be held again and that these critics *might* change their mind. In other words, the use of perfect aspect can be seen as a form of hedging, thereby inserting ambiguity into a text, allowing Blair to lessen the degree of certainty he is expressing, and effectively encoding lower levels of conviction.

Another common way of marking evidentiality in English is through the use of adverbs (Chafe 1986; Biber & Finegan 1989), including directly through *Hedges*, which is too infrequent in the corpus to allow for quantitative analysis, and **Downtoners** (e.g. *almost, nearly, only*), which are more common in Blair's fake news, and which were already discussed in relationship to information density. In general, however, downtoners are often used specifically to express uncertainty, as illustrated in examples 25 and 26.

25. *It was almost as if he wanted to talk about anything – anything other than his elder daughter.* (F24)

26. *San Jose State is among nearly a dozen universities that are trying to comply with a new N.C.A.A. minimum attendance rule for football programs in Division I-A.* (F05)

In example 25, Blair's use of the downtoner *almost* signals that he does not know exactly what Jessica Lynch's father wants to talk about, which must be the case, as he is essentially reporting here on someone else's mental state. Crucially, however, we know that Blair never actually met her father. It is also notable that the use of *almost* here is essentially redundant, as Blair also qualifies the statement with *as if*, perhaps reflecting an increased lack of confidence in this claim, compared to if he *had* met with Lynch's father. Similarly, in example 26, the downtoner *nearly* is used to mark a lack of specificity in the number of universities with this issue. Both of these usages effectively reduce the level of conviction being expressed by Blair.

The last feature that exhibits a non-negligible difference between Blair's real and fake news is WH Relatives *(Subject Gap)*. These are relative clauses that are used to post-modify a noun, generally a human or another animate entity, where the noun is associated with the subject of the embedded clause (Biber et al. 1999). In all but one of the 131 cases of this feature in the full corpus, the WH clause is headed by *who*. Surprisingly WH Relatives are more common in Blair's fake news, even though we might expect this feature to be more common in Blair's real news, as they are used to provide additional information about human nouns, as illustrated in examples 27 to 30.

27. *Jo-Ellan Dimitrius, a Los Angeles-based jury consultant who advised the defense team in the O. J. Simpson murder trial, said that she was not surprised by the legal challenge.* (R23)

28. *"There is not much pointing to Muhammad, and that is going to make it really hard to show that he was the triggerman," said one senior law enforcement official who is involved in the case.* (F11)

29. *The prisoners of war had already been identified by military officials and relatives who had seen their television images.* (F23)

30. *Muhammad was shown the soldier by a friend who was a doctor at the hospital, her relatives said today.* (F30)

In example 27, Blair uses the relative clause to add background information about a named expert, *Jo-Ellan Dimitrius*, who he then quotes indirectly. In example 28, Blair once again provides additional information about an expert source, *a senior law enforcement official*, who is now directly quoted, although the source is anonymous. Alternatively, in example 29, Blair provides additional information about a large group of *military officials and relatives* referenced in his story. Finally, in example 30, Blair provides information about an anonymous 'friend' referenced in an indirect quote from unnamed *relatives*.

To better understand variation in the use of relative clauses headed by *who* in our corpus, we considered variation in the 130 nouns being modified in Blair's real and fake news. We found that Blair uses WH Relatives 49 per cent of the time in his real news to provide additional information about specific people (i.e. who could be identified based on the information contained in the article), compared to 43 per cent of the time in his fake news. We also found that Blair uses WH Relatives 88 per cent of the time in his real news to provide additional information about nouns referencing experts and people with specific societal roles, compared to 67 per cent of the time in his fake news. For example, ignoring pluralisation, the expert nouns he most frequently modifies in this way in both real and fake news are *analyst*, *lawyer*, *officer*, *official*, and *prosecutor*. Alternatively, the only non-expert nouns Blair modifies in his real news are *person* (2), *guy*, and *man*, in addition to the pronoun *those*, whereas, in his fake news, he modifies *man* (8), *person* (4), *friend* (2), *Iraqi* (2), *other* (2), *woman (2), boy, brother, child, daughter, family, husband, kid, mother, relative, son,* and *uncle.* He also modifies *soldier* (6) and *marine* (4) in his fake news, but never in his real news. Blair is therefore not only using *WH Relatives* more often in his fake news, but he is using WH Relatives more often to provide additional information about non-experts, who often go unnamed, including both the people he is reporting on and the sources he is citing. Blair is therefore effectively spending more time providing information from and about non-specific and non-expert people in his fake news, leading to news that is less grounded in expert opinion and more difficult to validate. The more frequent use of WH Relatives in Blair's fake news therefore also reflects a lack of conviction.

5.3.3 Summary

The eight features discussed in this section differentiate between how Blair expresses his personal stance towards the information he is reporting in his real and fake news. In his real news, Blair writes with greater conviction: he writes with more certainty about the events he is reporting and their future relevance, and he identifies the people he is reporting on with more clarity and specificity. In terms of his sources, he is more specific about who they are and tends to place greater emphasis on the opinions of experts, sharing their reports with greater confidence. Alternatively, in his fake news, Blair writes with greater uncertainty, less likely to discuss the ramifications of the news he is reporting and more likely to hedge. He is also less specific about the people who he reports on and what they tell him. The explanation for this pattern appears to be straightforward: when Blair is telling the truth, he writes with detail and certainty; when he is lying, he consciously or unconsciously becomes less specific, making it difficult to interrogate or question the information he is sharing, ultimately resulting in a less confident and transparent style of reporting.

Overall, in this section, we have therefore identified two major patterns of stylistic variation in Blair's reporting based on an analysis of twenty-eight grammatical features that are commonly used in register analysis and whose relative frequencies differ substantially between Blair's real and fake news. Specifically, Blair writes real news in a more informationally dense and confident style, whereas he writes fake news in a less informationally dense and confident style. These patterns are complex, involving a large number of co-occurring grammatical features with varying communicative functions, but on the whole these two patterns are clear, and the way they differentiate between Blair's real and fake news can be linked directly to variation in Blair's production circumstances and communicative goals, as well as differences in the underlying status of the information he was communicating.

6 Conclusion

In this Element, we have introduced a framework for the linguistic analysis of fake news, drawing especially on insights from research on disinformation and register variation. Based on this framework, we have presented an analysis of variation in the linguistic structure of real and fake news written by Jayson Blair of *The New York Times*. Overall, we have identified specific grammatical patterns that distinguish between Blair's real and fake news, and we have proposed explanations for why these patterns exist. In this final section, we consider how our framework and our findings may extend our general understanding of fake news, after briefly summarising our main results.

Our study provides clear evidence of variation in Blair's style of writing when he is telling the truth and when he is lying. In general, Blair's real and fake news are written in a similar style that seems appropriate for newspaper writing. Adopting a professional and relatively consistent style is presumably one of the ways Blair was able to avoid detection for so long at one of the most important newspapers in the world. However, based on a quantitative corpus analysis of his use of forty-nine grammatical features, we found that the relative frequencies of twenty-eight of these features show substantial differences across twenty-eight real and thirty-six fake articles written by Blair over a six-month period. Furthermore, based on a qualitative discourse analysis of Blair's use of these twenty-eight features in our corpus, we identified two basic patterns of stylistic variation that we argue distinguish between his real and fake news: when Blair is telling the truth, his articles are characterised by higher levels of information density and conviction.

We have also argued that these differences in language use directly reflect differences in the communicative context in which Blair wrote real and fake news and his communicative intent. It appears Blair wrote fake news with lower levels of information density primarily because he was trying to write many articles quickly over short periods of time. An informationally dense style is generally associated with written registers, like newspaper writing, that focus on conveying large amounts of information in a limited space, and where authors crucially have time to edit carefully. Because Blair was writing fake news under pressure, it seems that he was not able to write as densely as he usually would. Furthermore, writing more densely would have only forced him to fabricate more information. Similarly, it appears Blair wrote fake news with less conviction because he knew he was communicating fabricated information, leading him to inadvertently mark his fake news for uncertainty.

In addition to describing how and why one journalist wrote fake news, we believe our framework and our study can also help extend our understanding of the phenomenon of fake news more generally. At the most basic level, this study provides strong evidence that the linguistic structure of real and fake news *can* vary in consistent and meaningful ways. In our opinion, this relationship has not been clearly established in previous research on the language of fake news, which has defined fake news in terms of veracity as opposed to deception, left important sources of linguistic variation uncontrolled, and failed to distinguish variation in language content from variation in linguistic structure. Alternatively, in this study, we have shown that systematic patterns of grammatical variation can differentiate between real and fake news that was knowingly written by one journalist, writing for one newspaper, over a short period of time.

Although we have only analysed the language of one author, it seems likely that this type of linguistic variation could differentiate between real and fake news more generally. Because all journalists who write real and fake news must share underlyingly the same opposing communicative goals – that is, to inform or deceive their readership – the linguistic structure of real and fake news should vary in systematic ways. Further empirical research is needed to validate this hypothesis and to test the strength and consistency of these patterns of linguistic variation across other authors, news registers, dialects, and languages, but we believe this basic insight can immediately begin to inform research in a range of fields that analyse fake news.

Most notably, we believe our study and our framework are relevant to research on fake news detection in natural language processing. This research has progressed under the assumption that variation exists in the language of real and fake news, despite very little data or theory to support this claim. Much research in modern natural language processing involves tasks we know humans can easily resolve like answering questions or summarising texts, arguably making empirical evidence that such tasks can be resolved through supervised machine learning unnecessary. Fake news detection, however, is different. Because humans, including Blair's editors at *The New York Times*, are bad at identifying fake news, we should not assume that a machine learning system can be trained to solve this task, especially if we lack an explanation for why differences should exist in the language of real and fake news. By providing a theoretical basis for the study of the language of fake news, this Element sets a foundation for future research on language-based fake news detection.

Specifically, this Element can inform data collection, data analysis, and data interpretation in research on fake news detection in natural language processing. In terms of data collection, we have highlighted issues with fake news corpora that are compiled by sampling real and fake news from incommensurable varieties of language and that define the difference between real and fake news in terms of veracity as opposed to deception. The standard approach in natural language processing allows for substantial training data to be collected and for good accuracy to be achieved, but it moves research away from the type of fake news that is difficult for humans to identify and that is of greatest societal concern (i.e. Type II Fake News). In terms of data analysis, we provide a set of grammatical features, drawn from register analysis, that could be incorporated into machine learning systems. This would seem to be especially useful for resolving the most challenging cases of fake news, where variation in content cannot be assumed to be correlated with variation in honesty. In terms of data interpretation, we have demonstrated how communicative context and purpose can provide a basis for explaining patterns of grammatical variation that distinguish between real and fake news, which is especially important for justifying real-world applications of fake news detection systems, where it is quite rightfully expected that the identification of fake news can be explained.

Although this study provides some evidence for the viability of automated fake news detection systems, as well as a number of general insights for the development of such tools, it is unclear whether the specific patterns of stylistic variation we have identified for Blair could be used to distinguish between real and fake news written by journalists more generally. Variation in information density appears to be largely explained by Blair having less time to edit his fake news, but we can imagine other contexts where individual fake news articles would be constructed with great care. Still, the challenge to express information efficiently is presumably a much greater problem for journalists who are telling the truth than for journalists who are lying, and low information density could therefore be a general marker of fake news. The expression of conviction would seem like an even better candidate for a general marker of fake news, as it is directly linked to a journalist's intent to deceive, which is exactly how we have defined fake news (i.e. in terms of disinformation as opposed to misinformation). Nevertheless, it would seem like there are many different reasons a journalist might lie, and many different ways they might go about doing it. Further empirical analysis of the language of fake news as written by many authors is necessary to resolve these types of questions, but if a range of different styles of fake news were described through large-scale corpus analysis, these results could potentially be used as the basis for more accurate and informative fake news detection systems.

We also believe our study can extend our understanding of the psychology of fake news – why journalists lie and why the public believes them. Crucially, the case of Jayson Blair demonstrates how very specific and personal factors can motivate a journalist to lie, while our analysis of his writings demonstrates how these types of factors can affect how a journalist writes. Because we can see a link between variation in Blair's communicative intent and variation in the style in which he wrote real and fake news, it may be possible more generally to infer the motivations of an author of fake news based on the style in which they write. If the measurement of variation in a journalist's style of writing can be used to assess a journalist's communicative intent, this could be the basis for large-scale language-based psychometric research on the motivations for the production of fake news.

Our study may also provide insight on why people believe fake news. Just as there are many reasons to lie, there are many reasons to believe a lie. People scrolling past clickbait on social media may be fooled because they do not take enough time to assess the post, but this does not explain why people reading Blair's articles for years at *The New York Times,* including his editors, were not able to identify his deception. It is unclear why Blair's fake news was so difficult to detect and to what extent this was linked to his style of writing, although certainly adopting an altogether different style when he wrote fake news would have attracted attention. Maybe Blair was good at maintaining a consistent style, with variation only detected in this study through careful linguistic analysis, or maybe he subtly varied his style to help conceal his deception. Understanding why Blair's style of fake news was so difficult to detect, and how readers judge the writing styles of Blair and other authors, could help us understand what makes people believe fake news – and possibly how to combat fake news at scale.

We should, however, question if the problem of fake news can truly be addressed through large-scale fake news detection. For human society to be affected by fake news, a human must process it and believe it. Judging the reliability of news is something that must be done every time anyone reads news, regardless of whether it has already been filtered for us by another person or a machine. In our opinion, the problem of fake news can only be truly addressed through the close, critical, and personal reading of the news. In this study, we have shown how to read Blair's news in great detail, and, although every journalist and every news item needs to be read on its own terms, insights from this study can inform this process, as can the methods of critical discourse analysis more generally, which have long been used to scrutinise the language of the news media and to reveal its hidden meanings and biases. People must learn to read the news with care and scepticism no matter where it comes from. This is not easy, but we are not born reading news, much less believing it. These are behaviours we learn, and we can learn other behaviours if we so choose.

Finally, this study highlights that deception occurs in the mainstream news media, not just on the fringes of the Internet. We do not know what proportion of fake news comes from different sources. It seems that fake news originating from outside the mainstream news media has increased dramatically over the past decade, due at least in part to the rise of digital communication and social media. But this should not be taken as evidence that the production of mainstream fake news has decreased, much less disappeared. In fact, it may well have increased, given growing demand for news and growing access to information online, which was already the basis for much of Blair's fake news two decades ago. Furthermore, societal concern over fake news originating from the periphery of the news media presumably makes it even easier for fake news to go undetected at its core. Coverage of the online fake news crisis by the mainstream media could even be used to divert attention from more institutionalised forms of disinformation.

Similar criticisms can be levelled against academic research on fake news. If machine learning systems are trained with mainstream news as the prototype for real news, or if mainstream news is ignored altogether, these systems cannot be expected to hold the news media accountable. This is unacceptable: fake news in the mainstream press is where the most societal damage can be done. For example, to take what is perhaps the most flagrant breach of the public's trust, during the lead up to the Iraq War in 2002, the mainstream press reported on the presence of weapons of mass destruction in Iraq, which we now know never existed. This was the justification for a war that has led to a massive loss of life. *The New York Times* was at the forefront of this innaccurate reporting, eventually issuing an official apology for their coverage in 2004. This was the newsroom where Blair learned his trade. In our opinion, his lies, minor by comparison, were a symptom of this greater culture of deception, not the cause. This is why we cannot trust the news media to address the problem of fake news. Independent and vigorous academic research is necessary to hold the news media accountable.

References

Aikhenvald, A. Y. (2004). *Evidentiality.* Oxford University Press.

Allcott, H., & Gentzkow, M. (2017). Social media and fake news in the 2016 election. *Journal of Economic Perspectives*, 31(2), 211–36.

Allen, R. J. (1993). Expertise and the Daubert decision. *Journal Criminal Law & Criminology*, 84, 1157.

Aslam, N., Khan, I. U., Alotaibi, F. S., Aldaej, L. A., & Aldubaikil, A. K. (2021). Fake detect: A deep learning ensemble model for fake news detection. *Complexity*, 2021, 5557784.

Asr, F. T., & Taboada, M. (2018). The data challenge in misinformation detection: Source reputation vs. content veracity. *Proceedings of the First Workshop on Fact Extraction and VERification (FEVER)*, 10–15.

Asr, F. T., & Taboada, M. (2019). Big data and quality data for fake news and misinformation detection. *Big Data & Society*, 6(1), 1–14.

Baayen, R. H. (2002). *Word Frequency Distributions*. Springer.

Barron, J. (1 December 2006). Respect and Regrets at Memorial for Times Editor. *The New York Times*. www.nytimes.com.

Barry, D., Barstow, D., Glater, J., Liptak, A., & Steinberg, J. (11 April 2003). Times Reporter Who Resigned Leaves Long Trail of Deception. *The New York Times*. www.nytimes.com.

Biber, D. (1988). *Variation across Speech and Writing*. Cambridge University Press.

Biber, D. (1995). *Dimensions of Register Variation: A Cross-linguistic Comparison*. Cambridge University Press.

Biber, D., & Conrad, S. (2019). *Register, Genre, and Style*. Cambridge University Press.

Biber, D., & Finegan, E. (1989). Styles of stance in English: Lexical and grammatical marking of evidentiality and affect. *Text*, 9(1), 93–124.

Biber, D., Gray, B., Staples, S., & Egbert, J. (2020). Investigating grammatical complexity in L2 English writing research: Linguistic description versus predictive measurement. *Journal of English for Academic Purposes*, *46*, 100869.

Biber, D., Johansson, S., Leech, G., Conrad, S., & Finegan, E. (1999). *Longman Grammar of Spoken and Written English*. Longman.

Blair, J. (2004). *Burning Down My Masters' House*. New Millennium Press.

Blanco-Gómez, M. L. (2002). Hiding the agent in English and Spanish newspaper articles: The periphrastic passive. In Juana, I. M. A. (ed.), *Conceptualization of Events in Newspaper Discourse: Mystification of Agency and Degree of Implication in News Reports* (pp. 9–30). Universidad Complutense de Madrid, Proyectos Complutense 2000, PR52/00–8888.

Boghardt, T. (2009). Soviet Bloc intelligence and its AIDS disinformation campaign. *Studies in Intelligence*, 53(4), 1–24.

Bondielli, A., & Marcelloni, F. (2019). A survey on fake news and rumour detection techniques. *Information Sciences*, 497, 38–55.

Bonet-Jover, A., Piad-Morffis, A., Saquete, E., Martínez-Barco, P., & García-Cumbreras, M. Á. (2021). Exploiting discourse structure of traditional digital media to enhance automatic fake news detection. *Expert Systems with Applications*, 169, 114340.

Calame, B. (18 June 2006). Preventing a Second Jayson Blair. *The New York Times*. www.nytimes.com.

Calderone, M. (31 May 2017). The New York Times Is Eliminating The Public Editor Role. *The Huffington Post*. www.huffingtonpost.co.uk.

Castelo, S., Almeida, T., Elghafari, A. et al. (2019). A topic-agnostic approach for identifying fake news pages. *Companion Proceedings of the 2019 World Wide Web Conference*, 975–980.

Chafe, W. (1982). Integration and involvement in speaking, writing, and oral literature. In D. Tannen (ed.), *Spoken and Written Language: Exploring Orality and Literacy* (pp. 35–53). Ablex.

Chafe, W. (1985). Linguistic differences produced by differences between speaking and writing. In D. R. Olson, N. Torrance, & A. Hildyard (eds.), *Literacy, Language, and Learning: The Nature and Consequences of Reading and Writing* (pp. 105–23). Cambridge University Press.

Chafe, W. (1986). Evidentiality in english conversation and academic writing. In W. Chafe, & J. Nichols (eds.), *Evidentiality: The Linguistic Coding of Epistemology* (pp. 261–72). Ablex.

Chafe, W., & Tannen, D. (1987). The relation between written and spoken language. *Annual Review of Anthropology*, 16(1), 383–407.

Cision Media Research. (2019). Top 10 U.S. Daily Newspapers. www.cision.com.

Cliff, N. (1993). Dominance statistics: Ordinal analyses to answer ordinal questions. *Psychological Bulletin*, 114(3), 494–509.

Conroy, N. J., Rubin, V. L., & Chen, Y. (2015). Automatic deception detection: Methods for finding fake news. *Proceedings of the Association for Information Science and Technology*, 52(1), 1–4.

Cull, N. J., Gatov, V., Pomerantsev, P., Applebaum, A., & Shawcross, A. (2017). *Soviet Subversion, Disinformation and Propaganda: How the West Fought against It*. LSE Consulting.

Del Vicario, M., Bessi, A., Zollo, F. et al. (2016). The spreading of misinformation online. *Proceedings of the National Academy of Sciences*, 113(3), 554–9.

Duxbury, S. W., Frizzell, L. C., & Lindsay, S. L. (2018). Mental illness, the media, and the moral politics of mass violence: The role of race in mass shootings coverage. *Journal of Research in Crime and Delinquency*, 55(6), 766–97.

Fallis, D. (2009). What is lying? *The Journal of Philosophy*, 106(1), 29–56.

Fetzer, J. H. (2004). Disinformation: The use of false information. *Minds and Machines*, 14(2), 231–40.

Gelfert, A. (2018). Fake news: A definition. *Informal Logic*, 38(1), 84–117.

Gray, B., & Biber, D. (2012). Current conceptions of stance. In K. Hyland & C. S. Guinda (eds.), *Stance and Voice in Written Academic Genres* (pp. 15–33). Palgrave Macmillan.

Grieve, J. (2007). Quantitative authorship attribution: An evaluation of techniques. *Literary and Linguistic Computing*, 22(3), 251–70.

Grieve, J. (2016). *Regional Variation in Written American English*. Cambridge University Press.

Grieve, J., Biber, D., Friginal, E., & Nekrasova, T. (2010). Variation among blogs: A multi-dimensional analysis. In A. Mehler, S. Sharoff, & M. Santini (eds.), *Genres on the Web* (pp. 303–22). Springer.

Grieve J., & Woodfield, H. (2020). Investigative linguistics. In M. Coulthard, A. May, & R. Sousa-Silva (eds.), *The Routledge Handbook of Forensic Linguistics* (pp. 660–74). Routledge.

Halliday, M. A. K. (1978). *Language as Social Semiotics*. Edward Arnold.

Herbert, B. (19 May 2003). Truth, Lies and Subtext. *The New York Times*. www .nytimes.com.

Hernandez, M. (18 April 2003a). Texas Soldier; Valley Mom Awaits News of MIA Son. *San Antonio Express-News*. www.expressnews.com.

Hernandez, M. (1 June 2003b). What Jayson Blair Stole From Me, and Why I Couldn't Ignore It. *The Washington Post*. www.washingtonpost.com.

Hindman, E. B. (2005). Jayson Blair, The New York Times, and paradigm repair. *Journal of Communication*, 55(2), 225–41.

Hollihan, T. A. (1984). Propagandizing in the interest of war: A rhetorical study of the committee on public information. *Southern Speech Communication Journal*, 49(3), 241–57.

Horne, B., & Adali, S. (2017). This just in: Fake news packs a lot in title, uses simpler, repetitive content in text body, more similar to satire than real news.

Proceedings of the International AAAI Conference on Web and Social Media, 11 (1), 759–66.

Igwebuike, E. E., & Chimuanya, L. (2021). Legitimating falsehood in social media: A discourse analysis of political fake news. *Discourse & Communication*, 15(1), 42–58.

Infelise, M. (2002). Roman avvisi: Information and politics in the seventeenth century. In G. Signorotto, & M. A. Visceglia (eds.), *Court and Politics in Papal Rome* (pp. 212–28). Cambridge University Press.

Izvorski, R. (1997). The present perfect as an epistemic modal. *Semantics and Linguistic Theory*, 7, 222–39.

Kang, C. (21 November 2016). Fake News Onslaught Targets Pizzeria as Nest of Child-trafficking. *The New York Times*. www.nytimes.com.

Keller, B. (9 May 2005). Times Editor's Response to Credibility Report. *The New York Times*. www.nytimes.com.

Kelley, T. (13 May 2003). Times Editor Details Steps to Prevent a Recurrence of Fraud. *The New York Times*. www.nytimes.com.

Kurtz, H. (30 April 2003a). New York Times Story Gives Texas Paper Sense of Deja Vu. *The Washington Post*. www.washingtonpost.com.

Kurtz, H. (2 May 2003b). Reporter Resigns Over Copied Story. *The Washington Post*. www.washingtonpost.com.

Kurtz, H. (10 May 2003c). Disgraced Reporter's Deceptions Date to '99. *The Washington Post*. www.washingtonpost.com.

Kurtz, H. (11 May 2003d). N.Y. Times Uncovers Dozens Of Faked Stories by Reporter. *The Washington Post*. www.washingtonpost.com.

Kurtz, H. (12 May 2003e). Top Gun, Bottom Line. *The Washington Post*. www.washingtonpost.com.

Lazer, D. M., Baum, M. A., Benkler, Y. et al. (2018). The science of fake news. *Science*, 359, 1094–6.

Leo, J. (18 May 2003). Relaxed Standards Undermine Journalism. *Lewiston Sun Journal*. www.sunjournal.com.

Lin, J., Tremblay-Taylor, G., Mou, G., You, D., & Lee, K. (2019). Detecting fake news articles. *2019 IEEE International Conference on Big Data (Big Data)*, 3021–3025.

Magden, D. (19 May 2003). Former Times Liar Battles Coke: Mags. *New York Post*. https://nypost.com.

Mangal, D., & Sharma, D. K. (2021). A framework for detection and validation of fake news via authorize source matching. In *Micro-Electronics and Telecommunication Engineering* (pp. 577–86). Springer, Singapore.

Mitra, T., & Gilbert, E. (2015). Credbank: A large-scale social media corpus with associated credibility annotations. *Proceedings of the Ninth International AAAI Conference on Web and Social Media*, 258–67.

Mnookin, S. (2004). *Hard News: Scandals at* The New York Times *and Their Meaning for American Media*. Random House.

New York Times. (11 May 2003a). Editor's Note. *The New York Times*. www .nytimes.com.

New York Times. (11 May 2003b). Witnesses and Documents Unveil Deceptions in a Reporter's Work. www.nytimes.com.

New York Times. (26 May 2004). The Times and Iraq. *The New York Times*. www.nytimes.com.

Newsweek. (18 May 2003). A Journalist's Hard Fall. *Newsweek*. www .newsweek.com.

Nini, A. (2019). The multi-dimensional analysis tagger. In T. Berber Sardinha, & M. Veirano Pinto (eds.), *Multi-Dimensional Analysis: Research Methods and Current Issues* (pp. 67–94). Bloomsbury Academic.

Oshikawa, R., Qian, J., & Wang, W. Y. (2020). A survey on natural language processing for fake news detection. *Proceedings of the 12th Language Resources and Evaluation Conference*, 6086–93.

Patterson, M. J., & Urbanski, S. (2006). What Jayson Blair and Janet Cooke say about the press and the erosion of public trust. *Journalism Studies*, 7(6), 828–50.

Pennycook, G., & Rand, D. G. (2019). Lazy, not biased: Susceptibility to partisan fake news is better explained by lack of reasoning than by motivated reasoning. *Cognition*, 188, 39–50.

Pennycook, G., & Rand, D. G. (2021). The psychology of fake news. *Trends in Cognitive Sciences*, 25(5), 388–402.

Pérez-Rosas, V., Kleinberg, B., Lefevre, A., & Mihalcea, R. (2018). Automatic detection of fake news. *Proceedings of the 27th International Conference on Computational Linguistics*, 3391–3401.

Picornell, I. (2013). Analysing deception in written witness statements. *Linguistic Evidence in Security, Law and Intelligence*, 1(1), 41–50.

Potthast, M., Kiesel, J., Reinartz, K., Bevendorff, J., & Stein, B. (2017). A stylometric inquiry into hyperpartisan and fake news. *Proceedings of the 56th Annual Meeting of the Association for Computational Linguistics (Volume 1: Long Papers)*, 231–240.

Rashkin, H., Choi, E., Jang, J. Y., Volkova, S., & Choi, Y. (2017). Truth of varying shades: Analyzing language in fake news and political fact-checking. *Proceedings of the 2017 Conference on Empirical Methods in Natural Language Processing*, 2931–7.

Robinson, P. (2017). Learning from the chilcot report: Propaganda, deception and the 'war on terror'. *International Journal of Contemporary Iraqi Studies*, 11, 47–73.

Romano, J., Kromrey, J. D., Coraggio, J., & Skowronek, J. (2006). Appropriate statistics for ordinal level data: Should we really be using t-test and Cohen's d for evaluating group differences on the NSSE and other surveys. *Annual Meeting of the Florida Association of Institutional Research*, 1–33.

Rubin, V. L. (2019). Disinformation and misinformation triangle: A conceptual model for 'fake news' epidemic, causal factors and interventions. *Journal of Documentation*, 75(5), 1013–34.

Rubin, V. L., Chen, Y., & Conroy, N. K. (2015). Deception detection for news: Three types of fakes. *Proceedings of the Association for Information Science and Technology*, 52(1), 1–4.

Safire, W. (12 May 2003). Huge Black Eye. *The New York Times*. www.nytimes.com.

Santia, G. C., & Williams, J. R. (2018). Buzzface: A news veracity dataset with Facebook user commentary and egos. *Twelfth International AAAI Conference on Web and Social Media*, 531–40.

Scocca, T. (29 May 2006). Man Who Knew Plenty: Times' Siegal Imprinted Invisibly on Newspaper. *Observer*. https://observer.com.

Shafer, J. (14 March 2004). Dateline: Brooklyn. *The New York Times*. www.nytimes.com.

Shu, K., Mahudeswaran, D., Wang, S., Lee, D., & Liu, H. (2020). Fakenewsnet: A data repository with news content, social context, and spatiotemporal information for studying fake news on social media. *Big Data*, 8(3), 171–88.

Shu, K., Sliva, A., Wang, S., Tang, J., & Liu, H. (2017). Fake news detection on social media: A data mining perspective. *ACM SIGKDD Explorations Newsletter*, 19(1), 22–36.

Silverman, C., Lytvynenko, J., Vo, L. T., & Singer-Vine, J. (8 August 2017). Inside the partisan fight for your news feed. *Buzzfeed News*. www.buzzfeednews.com/article/craigsilverman/inside-the-partisan-fight-for-your-news-feed.

Spayd, L. (2 June 2017). The Public Editor Signs Off. *The New York Times*. www.nytimes.com.

Spurlock, J. (2016). Why journalists lie: The troublesome times for Janet Cooke, Stephen Glass, Jayson Blair, & Brian Williams. *ETC: A Review of General Semantics*, 73(1), 71–6.

Stahl, B. C. (2006). On the difference or equality of information, misinformation, and disinformation: A critical research perspective. *Informing Science: The International Journal of an Emerging Transdiscipline*, 9, 83–96.

Steinberg, J. (2 May 2003a). Times Reporter Resigns After Questions on Article. *The New York Times*. www.nytimes.com.

Steinberg, J. (15 May 2003b). Editor of Times Tells Staff He Accepts Blame for Fraud. *The New York Times*. www.nytimes.com.

Steinberg, J. (31 July 2003b). Times Editor to Select Reader Representative. *The New York Times*. www.nytimes.com.

Steinberg, J. (10 September 2003d). Times Names First Editor For Standards. *The New York Times*. www.nytimes.com.

Strauss, L. (1952). *Persecution and the Art of Writing*. The University of Chicago Press.

Tagliamonte, S. A. (2006). *Analysing Sociolinguistic Variation*. Cambridge University Press.

Tandoc Jr, E. C., Lim, Z. W., & Ling, R. (2018). Defining 'fake news' A typology of scholarly definitions. *Digital Journalism*, 6(2), 137–53.

Torchiano, M. (2020). Effsize: Efficient Effect Size Computation. R package version 0.80. https://cran.r-project.org/web/packages/effsize/index.html.

van Der Linden, S., Roozenbeek, J., & Compton, J. (2020). Inoculating against fake news about COVID-19. *Frontiers in Psychology*, 11, 2928.

van Dijk, T. A. (1983). Discourse analysis: Its development and application to the structure of news. *Journal of Communication*, 33(2), 20–43.

Vlachos, A., & Riedel, S. (2014). Fact checking: Task definition and dataset construction. *Proceedings of the ACL 2014 Workshop on Language Technologies and Computational Social Science*, 18–22.

Wang, W. Y. (2017). 'Liar, Liar Pants on Fire': A New Benchmark Dataset for Fake News Detection. *Proceedings of the 55th Annual Meeting of the Association for Computational Linguistics (Volume 2: Short Papers)*, 422–6.

Wenzel, A. (2019). To verify or to disengage: Coping with 'fake news' and ambiguity. *International Journal of Communication*, *13*, 1977–95.

Woo, W. (15 September 2003). The Siegal Committee Report. *Nieman Reports*. https://niemanreports.org.

World Health Organization. (2020). *Coronavirus disease (COVID-19) advice for the public: Mythbusters*. www.who.int/emergencies/diseases/novel-coronavirus-2019/advice-for-public/myth-busters.

Yagoda, B. (2006). *When You Catch an Adjective Kill It: Parts of Speech, for Better And/Or Worse*. Broadway Books.

Yagoda, B. (11 March 2007). When You Catch an Adjective, Kill It. *The New York Times*. www.nytimes.com.

Zhou, X., & Zafarani, R. (2020). A survey of fake news: Fundamental theories, detection methods, and opportunities. *ACM Computing Surveys (CSUR)*, 53 (5), 1–40.

Acknowledgements

We would like to thank Silje Alvestad, Matteo Fuoli, Tammy Gales, Tim Grant, Susan Hunston, Robbie Love, Liam McCarthy, Leonie Macdonald, Andrea Nini, Nele Põldvere, Emily Waibel, Amanda Woodfield, Hannah Woodfield, Richard Woodfield, Shirley Woodfield, and two anonymous reviewers for their input and support.

Cambridge Elements ☰

Forensic Linguistics

Tim Grant

Aston University

Tim Grant is Professor of Forensic Linguistics, Director of the Aston Institute for Forensic Linguistics, and past president of the International Association of Forensic Linguists. His recent publications have focussed on online sexual abuse conversations including Language and Online Identities: The Undercover Policing of Internet Sexual Crime (with Nicci MacLeod, Cambridge, 2020).

Tim is one of the world's most experienced forensic linguistic practitioners and his case work has involved the analysis of abusive and threatening communications in many different contexts including investigations into sexual assault, stalking, murder, and terrorism. He also makes regular media contributions including presenting police appeals such as for the BBC Crimewatch programme.

Tammy Gales

Hofstra University

Tammy Gales is an Associate Professor of Linguistics and the Director of Research at the Institute for Forensic Linguistics, Threat Assessment, and Strategic Analysis at Hofstra University, New York. She has served on the Executive Committee for the International Association of Forensic Linguists (IAFL), is on the editorial board for the peer-reviewed journals Applied Corpus Linguistics and Language and Law / Linguagem e Direito, and is a member of the advisory board for the BYU Law and Corpus Linguistics group. Her research interests cross the boundaries of forensic linguistics and language and the law, with a primary focus on threatening communications. She has trained law enforcement agents from agencies across Canada and the U.S. and has applied her work to both criminal and civil cases.

About the Series

Elements in Forensic Linguistics provides high-quality accessible writing, bringing cutting-edge forensic linguistics to students and researchers as well as to practitioners in law enforcement and law. Elements in the series range from descriptive linguistics work, documenting a full range of legal and forensic texts and contexts; empirical findings and methodological developments to enhance research, investigative advice, and evidence for courts; and explorations into the theoretical and ethical foundations of research and practice in forensic linguistics.

Cambridge Elements ☰

Forensic Linguistics

Printed in the United States
by Baker & Taylor Publisher Services